WEYMOUTH
More Golden Years

A COMPANION VOLUME TO *WEYMOUTH: THE GOLDEN YEARS*

PHOTOGRAPHS BY GRAHAM HERBERT

INTRODUCTION & CAPTIONS BY MAUREEN ATTWOOLL

DORSET BOOKS

First published in 2002 by Dorset Books
Reprinted in 2002, 2003
Image Copyright © 2002 Dorset County Council
Text Copyright © 2002 Maureen Attwooll

ISBN 1 871164 51 6

British Library Cataloguing-in-Publication-Data
A CIP data for this book is available from the British Library

DORSET BOOKS
Official publisher to Dorset County Council
Halsgrove House
Lower Moor Way
Tiverton EX16 6SS
T: 01884 243242
F: 01884 243325
www.halsgrove.com

Printed and bound in Great Britain by Bookcraft, Midsomer Norton

✑ CONTENTS ✑

ACKNOWLEDGEMENTS

I have received a great deal of assistance in preparing *Weymouth – More Golden Years*. One of the most enjoyable aspects of working in local history is that so many people are prepared to share their knowledge of the town and its past. Over the years so many people have contributed to my own knowledge of Weymouth that it is impossible to name everyone, but I do thank very sincerely all those who have shared their memories with me.

Special thanks regarding *Weymouth – More Golden Years* are due to:

Jack West who voluntarily undertook the huge task of indexing the Herbert negatives in his retirement. Without his input the task of compiling the book would have been almost impossible.

Brian Jackson, transport historian, whose help and advice on matters regarding the harbour, shipping and transport generally have been invaluable.

Ruth Lawrence, Graham Herbert's daughter, who provided me with the details of her late father's career.

Sue Wright, who took on the unenviable task of transcribing my longhand notes to produce the finished manuscript in record time.

Profolab of Weymouth, where the splendid photographs from the Herbert negatives were printed.

And to my husband, David Attwooll, who patiently accompanied me around the borough to identify locations, many of which had changed almost beyond recognition in the latter half of the twentieth century.

My thanks for help in providing information about individual photographs are due to Doug Hollings, Richard Jackson, Stella Knight, Bill Macey, Jeannette Matthews, members of the Dorset Transport Circle, Tarps Randall, residents of Chickerell, Wendy Webb.

INTRODUCTION

My task has been to select and caption the 300-plus pictures included in this second volume of Graham Herbert's superb photographs. I have been much influenced by reactions to the first volume of pictures and I have included additional illustrations of scenes which have proved to be of special interest, such as the floods of 1955 and the 1960s demolitions along High Street and North Quay. Events which featured local people evoked many memories and there are more of these in this collection.

The 1950s predominate, a decade of contrasts as the country struggled to overcome the ravages of war, yet displayed a determination to get back to normal and enjoy the pleasures of seaside holidays once again. It was a time of great change and we live today in a time of ever more rapid change and redevelopment. I have, for ease of recognition, included the names of today's occupants of various business premises in the town, but some of these were changing even as this book was being compiled.

Graham Valentine Herbert AIBP, ARPS
1911–1983

Graham Valentine Herbert was born in Walton-on-Thames, Surrey in 1911, the youngest of three children, having a brother Donald and a sister Gladys. The family moved to Weymouth in 1923, their father establishing the photographic business S.J. Herbert & Sons in the town, operating from a shop in Coburg Place at the top end of St Thomas Street. As a professional photographer Graham volunteered for the RAF on the outbreak of the Second World War and worked in the photographic section, mainly in Italy and North Africa. He returned to the family business after the war and it is from his surviving post-war negatives that the photographs for this book have been chosen. Some 300 Herbert pictures have already appeared in the first volume of *Weymouth – The Golden Years*, published in 2001, and this is a second selection from the negatives of the town and surrounding area. The photographs provide an unrivalled record of life in post-Second World War Weymouth.

Graham Herbert was a highly respected photographer and a popular citizen of the town. His interests outside photography included old time dancing, the Weymouth Operatic Society and Weymouth Rotary Club.

When he died in 1983, his widow Mollie presented his collection of negatives to Weymouth Library, an invaluable archive from which these selections have been made.

CHAPTER ONE

∾ TOWN TALK ∾

Shopping, street scenes and events

A very recognisable scene as this view takes us over the Town Bridge and into St Thomas Street – but there have been some changes here since 1956. Pankhurst's motorcycle showrooms were in the former Palladium cinema (now the Rendezvous Club). Next door, Marcelle the hairdresser and Dennett's fruit and veg shop have become the Marlboro fish and chip restaurant. Ward's store in St Edmund Street extended to the corner of St Thomas Street. Beyond it, the block occupied by Darch's cycle shop and the Swan Inn was pulled down in 1975 and the site has been extensively redeveloped. Then, as now, there were two bus stops on the Town Bridge but waiting passengers in the 1950s had no shelter whatsoever at this windy spot.

The Swan Inn, Town Bridge Café and Darch's shops (all now demolished) are on the left of this view looking down St Thomas Street in 1964. On the opposite side the occupants of all the shop premises shown have changed. They were (from right): Speedeluxe the dry cleaner, the Trustee Savings Bank, the *Dorset Evening Echo* office, grocer Guppy, grocer Northover and electrical engineers Davis & Hadley.

Northovers at No. 54 St Thomas Street went 'self-service' in 1967…

…prior to this, the old-fashioned shop seen here…

…had a wonderful system of conveying the customer's payment to the cashier at the rear of the shop via a system of pulleys and cables which similarly brought the change winging its way back to the assistant to complete the transaction.

Northover's new delivery vehicle, a Commer 1½-ton forward control van JJT 467, in 1956. Although the everyday use of the motor vehicle is now commonplace it has not meant an extended service to the customer and the number of tradesmen delivering on a regular basis has diminished over the years. The phrase 'Families waited on daily' has been consigned to the history book. Family grocers Northovers took pride in their service to customers and as well as the St Thomas Street shop, the firm was also at 85/87 High Street, Wyke Regis.

A typical but uninspiring 1960s reconstruction in St Thomas Street as Southern Gas wait to move out of Porter's old shop and into new showrooms next door. This street scene prior to rebuilding can be found in *Weymouth: The Golden Years*, page 73.

NatWest Bank (then National Provincial) has expanded since this picture was taken in 1956 and now includes Gregory the chemist's shop next door. Until the early 1900s chemist Gregory had occupied the whole of the corner site in St Thomas Street before he sold the bulk of it to the Devon & Cornwall Bank (later Lloyds), builders of this imposing Edwardian financial house.

Two national events in one month provided ideal material for a topical window display in 1960. Biles Bros at 87 St Thomas Street showed a range of magazines, books and jigsaws commemorating the forthcoming wedding of HRH Princess Margaret and Antony Armstrong-Jones, later Lord Snowdon. The same month, May, saw the FA Cup Final between Blackburn Rovers and Wolverhampton Wanderers, with suitable sporting merchandise on show. (Final score: Blackburn Rovers 0, Wolverhampton Wanderers 3). Biles' shop is now occupied by estate agent Connells.

No. 11 Frederick Place, St Thomas Street, Weymouth. During the years of 'Royal Weymouth' King George III's Gloucester Lodge gardens extended as far south as this terrace. Built on the former royal land in 1834, the property still retains most of its original features. It was once the office of local solicitor William Thompson, the Dorset-born pioneering photographer who is credited with having taken the world's first known underwater photograph, at Ferrybridge in 1856. A plaque commemorating his achievement was unveiled on the building in 1997.

The death of Sir Winston Churchill on 24 January 1965 was followed by a state funeral. Memorial services for the country's wartime Prime Minister were held all over Dorset and many shops and businesses mounted commemorative displays. Herbert exhibited crêpe-backed photographs of Churchill in panels on the front of his shop in St Thomas Street. The two ladies looking in the main window have obviously spotted someone they recognise in a montage of local wedding pictures.

A 1960 town-centre view which can today be more easily recognised at first-floor level. Eldridge Pope's Wines & Spirits shop (formerly trading under the name E. Browne & Co) was taken over by Meridian Shoes in 1999. Next door at No. 6, Southam's soft furnishings was to occupy the former Heron's premises (as well as No. 7) for more than twenty years. When the business closed, Brown the optician moved up the street to take over Nos 6 and 7.

A new contemporary look for the Co-op fish shop at 12 St Thomas Street in 1957.

Apart from the removal of traffic, for St Thomas Street was pedestrianised in the 1990s, the most notice-able change in this street scene from 1965 has been the demolition of three single-storey units on the right-hand side of the picture. Nos 81 to 83, the Gaumont cinema entrance, Comptons and The Bazaar had been built in front of the Old Rectory, almost completely concealing the imposing Georgian building which had once housed incumbents of St Mary's, the Parish Church. Since their removal, the rectory has been superbly restored and converted to a wine bar, attractively set back from the street. Comptons the stationers, when their shop at No 82 was due for demolition, moved 'up the road' and now occupy the former fruit and veg shop, A1 Stores.

Inevitably, all change once again at street level in the forty or so years since these shops were photographed in St Thomas Street. Marrs stocked high-fashion shoes, Roberts offered a range of delectable confectionery and Bakers supplied gifts and stationery for everyone. In 2002 two of these premises are occupied by estate agents and Roberts' shop stands empty.

A.F. Baker (in the previous photograph) occupied part of this fine block on the corner of St Thomas Street and St Alban Street. Adjoining shops in the 1960s were Shelley Roberts, chemist, and Templeman's shoes. Today, much plate glass has replaced the earlier shop fronts but the floors above retain the architecture of an earlier, more elegant age.

Roberts sold 'Boiled Sugars of Quality' – these glacé mints (8d a quarter) were produced at the firm's factory in Lower St Alban Street. Weymouth rock was another speciality among Roberts' tempting array of sweets.

It is still possible to park in St Nicholas Street but today's car park has extended south, closer to the harbour. The site shown here is now filled by the Lakeside Superbowl. This 1959 photograph looks towards West Street and Commercial Road and across the inner harbour to the industries of Westwey Road where the tall chimney of the former electricity generating station has now gone (demolished in 1974) but the gasometer remains, a reminder that this was once the site of Weymouth Gasworks. West Street and Commercial Road have changed almost beyond recognition. Practically all the buildings shown here have disappeared, to be replaced by tall apartment blocks and new terraced houses. The wall shown on the left-hand side of the photograph was part of local butcher Hurdle's slaughterhouse in St Nicholas Street.

A glance along St Nicholas Street in 1965 as the new Telephone Exchange goes up alongside the towering White Ensign Club. The club (opened in 1907 as the Sailors' Home) closed in 1965 owing to dwindling numbers of sailors using it and the maintenance costs of running the huge building. It was demolished in 1970 to make way for a supermarket which in turn made way for the present multiplex cinema. In St Alban Street a row of terraced houses was pulled down where the GPO Sorting Office and Telephone Exchange now stand. Beyond the Sorting Office under construction can be seen Webb Major's workshops and yard which were on the site of the present multi-storey car park.

The Golden Lion at the junction of St Mary Street and St Edmund Street is an old coaching inn. A 1798 guidebook advertised it as being kept by Mr W. Slyfield 'who has neat Post Chaises and careful Drivers'. Twentieth-century tales of the 'lion's tail' are described in *Weymouth: The Golden Years*, page 77. Next-door occupants of the 'round house' in 1958 were bakers Ferris and the Dorset Tool Company, founded by the Paddock family in 1933. The firm took over the baker's shop in 1959. Around the corner in St Mary Street was another long-established local family firm – photographers Kestins.

St Mary's Church in 1958. The scene is little changed today, although the road surface is now paved and the street pedestrianised. The post-war Market House in the background has been modernised and renamed Brenda Dench House in memory of one of the town's twentieth-century mayors. Shops in the foreground (right) were Foyles the grocer and shoe chain Bata.

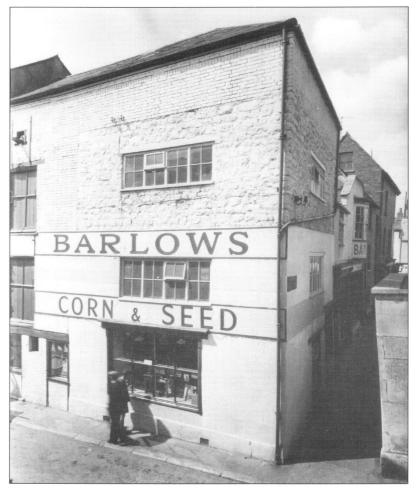

This narrow lane, Church Passage, runs along the side of St Mary's Church and links Maiden Street and St Mary Street. Corn and seed merchants Barlows occupied several buildings here in 1954, extending along the passage and also into an adjoining warehouse in Maiden Street. The Porthole restaurant currently occupies the corner site, the premises only slightly altered and still very recognisable.

Church Passage, looking towards Maiden Street.

At the lower end of St Mary Street, opposite St Mary's churchyard could be found Montague Burton. The 'tailor of taste' occupied Nos 62 and 62A in 1958. The tiled façade was very much in the style of the 1920s when Burton's arrived in the town. The tailors were here until the 1970s, the shop becoming two separate units in later years. 'Pop' Spetch's upstairs billiards saloon closed in 1961 and is now office space. The building has lost its Greek key cornice and rooftop advertising plaque. Current ground-floor occupants are a YMCA charity shop and Adams childrenswear.

Boots the chemists occupied Nos 69 and 70 St Mary Street and this photograph shows the store as refurbished in 1968. Many will remember 'Boots Booklovers' Library' on the first floor which closed in the mid-sixties. Following the company's amalgamation with the Timothy Whites & Taylors chain, the two stores swapped premises in the town, Boots moving to the larger shop at 81–82 St Mary Street. Timothy Whites' hardware stores eventually closed countrywide and this building is now occupied by Argos. Neighbours in the 1960s were local butcher Lawson Jones and Read the outfitter, supplier of countless school uniforms over the years.

A street scene which reflects some of the changes in shopping habits since 1965. MacFisheries (left) was one of three town-centre fresh-fish shops. John Collier was one of half a dozen gents tailors and there were a dozen small grocers' shops such as Pearks (far right). Today (from left) Nos 25-30 St Mary Street are occupied by a charity shop, Radio Rentals, Evans ladies' wear, a mobile phone shop and Crusty's bakery/café.

John Vincent, at No 86 St Mary Street was the town's leading jeweller, established in pre-Victorian times. Although today the shop's ground floor has been taken over by the inevitable plate glass (now Next), the upper floors, undergoing restoration in this 1957 picture, are still an elegant reminder of times past. Opposite was Maryon, a fashionable dress shop later taken over by its next-door neighbour H. Samuel.

Vincent's was well known for its dazzling window displays of silver plate and jewellery. This was a 1953 Coronation display – the draped fabric in the window is suitably printed with the royal coat of arms and 'Elizabeth R' monogram.

Bookseller and stationer Harry Wheeler's family had also been trading in Weymouth since Victorian times. The shop originally occupied Nos 20–21 St Mary Street but by the time of this 1958 photograph jeweller H. Samuel had taken over No. 20. The firm went on to add two more shops to its Weymouth store – No. 18, on the corner of Bond Street and St Mary Street and No. 21, Wheeler's, shown here.

Wheeler's incorporated into the H. Samuel shop. Heming & Tudor (No. 18) would be added later. Sporting in the sixties the then fashionable mosaic-effect shopfront, Samuel's façade is now painted a pale cream, blending with the earlier elegance of its bow-windowed first floor.

St Mary Street, looking north, in 1953, the scene dominated by the striking art deco architecture of F.W. Woolworth's store which seemed not at all out of place alongside the street's older buildings. Woolies' tiled façade was a great loss to the street scene in the late 1980s when it was replaced by a row of modern shop units. South of Woolworths, shopfronts have altered but the upper floors of these premises remain almost unchanged. At No. 15 was one of the 'outposts' of V.H. Bennett's large department store (the main store was in the left of the picture, now occupied by W.H. Smith and QS). No. 15 is now Barratt's shoeshop. At No. 16 was Lovell's Creameries (Roseby's today). Johnson Bros (cleaners and dyers) and Marcus the photographer were at No. 17 (now a mobile phone shop). The Midland Bank has changed only its name – to HSBC.

St Mary Street in 1962, with Woolworth's in the background. The shoppers are gazing into the windows of Lovell's Creameries Ltd. Although he probably did not realise it at the time, the patient gentleman on the right is carrying the trademark of the sixties' shopper – the wicker 'gondola' basket (as is one of the ladies in the photograph). When Woolworth's closed in 1982 it was lost to the town for some years but a new store opened in the New Bond Street development in 1999.

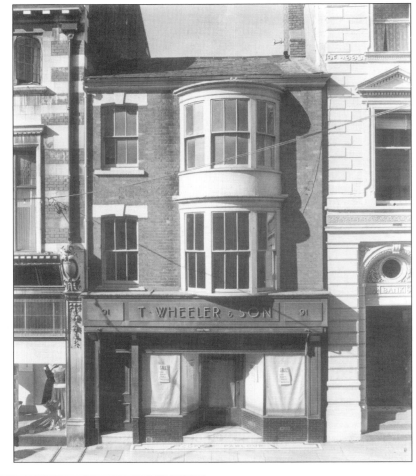

One building – 91 St Mary Street – with a change of occupants and appearance. This was No. 91 in 1956. T. Wheeler & Son, tea and coffee dealers and confectioners, had closed, selling their entire stock, fixtures and fittings. It was an attractive little bow-windowed building standing between its taller neighbours, V.H. Bennett's department store and Lloyds Bank.

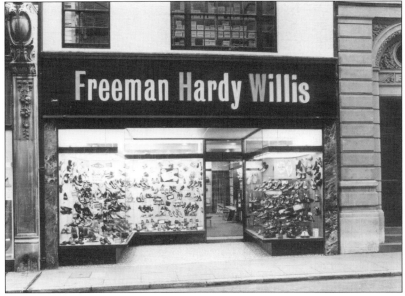

A year later, and the new occupants of the shop – shoe retailers Freeman Hardy Willis had redesigned the ground floor of No. 91 to include more window space for their displays. It is rather a shame that two of Weymouth's 'signature' bow windows were removed at first and second-floor levels. No. 91 is currently occupied by Clinton Cards. The ornate carved column on Bennett's shop still remains (W.H. Smith today).

A most extraordinary architectural design at No. 104 St Mary Street (opposite Marks & Spencer). Its façade includes two beautifully detailed creatures over the rainwater heads (are they dragons?), yet the building was only put up in 1926 for International Stores, grocers and tea dealers. The 1950s photograph was taken just after the shop had been converted to self-service. Next-door neighbour Meech the outfitter has since taken over No. 104.

A glimpse of St Alban Street in 1961. Joe Edge the bookmaker was in premises above the Civil & Military Stores (an independent unit, not part of the big London shop). Further up the street the tall building on the right housed Sutton's Grocery Stores, still trading as a coffee house under the Sutton name. Today this is one of Weymouth's most picturesque thoroughfares, leading to the seafront.

Such an attractive corner of Old Melcombe – Ye Olde Sally Lunne Shoppe on the corner of St Alban Street and Maiden Street – then, as now, a baker's shop. St Alban Street took on its present name in the mid-nineteenth century, prior to which it was known as Petticoat Lane.

These buildings behind the town's busy main street are little changed today. In 1955 Dupont Bros. Ltd occupied 9 Market Street. The firm sold clothing for cash as well as on the never-never, a deposit securing the required item for which the customer paid instalments each week. Present tenants are Fish & Fritz. Next door in Maiden Street is the Market House Tavern, taking its name from the nearby Victorian Market House which stood in St Mary Street until 1939. In the town's early history this area close to the harbour was the site of the traditional twice-weekly markets (Tuesdays and Fridays).

Close! A van negotiates a tight turn from School Street into Great George Street in 1957. The building on the left is St Mary's School, founded in the early nineteenth century. In the late twentieth century demand for primary school places in the town centre fell and several closed down, including St Mary's in 1982. At the end of the decade a new Weymouth Library rose on the site, opened by HRH The Princess Royal on 8 November 1990.

The New Bridge Hotel has closed and today awaits conversion to housing. Beyond the hotel can just be seen the big sheds of Betts' timber yard, since demolished to provide the site of Park Street car park.

A once-familiar site as the boat train makes its way along Commercial Road in 1965, past the tall sheds of the timber yard. Progress was slow and often halted by those who parked close to the lines, seemingly oblivious to warning signs and No Parking notices. Perhaps visitors found it hard to believe that a full-size train was likely to trundle through the streets of a busy seaside town.

A photograph of 24 and 24A Westham Road, newly opened in June 1954. The two shops which formerly occupied this site – Oatey's fruit and veg store and Harry Balem, the next-door butcher – were rebuilt as one spacious shop, now Sew 'n' Sews.

The Candy Stores, No. 20 Westham Road, in 1954.

A night-time view (probably taken to illustrate new street lighting). It shows a Westham Road building which still exists, although altered beyond recognition. On the right are the Weymouth & District Co-operative Society's central premises in the town as opened in 1926. By the late 1950s the store was described as 'cumbersome, crowded and dark', and modernisation began. The £100,000 transformation included the installation of standard department-store plate-glass windows, the result of which can be seen in *Weymouth: The Golden Years*, page 86.

Inside the modernised Co-op store in Westham Road. Wilkinson's now occupy these premises.

CHAPTER TWO

PROM AND PARK

Happy holidays in old-fashioned style

A 1958 view showing the first terrace at the southern end of the Esplanade, with cranes installed on the £70,000 reconstructed harbour stage. Devonshire Buildings was originally completed in 1812 with a conventional squared-off end-of-terrace house, but the owners were persuaded to rebuild it with the rounded end shown, to match the other 'roundhouses' in the town. The land on which this terrace and adjoining Pulteney Buildings stand was reclaimed from the sea in the early 1800s.

The main entrance to the Alexandra Gardens Theatre was opposite Pulteney Buildings. Built in 1924, the theatre was taken over during the Second World War as part of the shore-based HMS *Bee*, a working up base for coastal forces, prior to its occupation by HMS (later USS) *Grasshopper* in preparation for the D-Day landings. Once derequisitioned, the theatre's programme of summer shows recommenced. In the early 1960s competition from the new Pavilion Theatre on the pier and the popularity of television, led to its closure and the theatre was converted to an amusements centre. The building was destroyed by fire in the autumn of 1993 and a new amusements complex has been erected on the site.

The Baptist congregation first worshipped in this building in 1814, but its appearance was very different then. The terms of the lease stipulated that no changes should be made to the exterior of the building, which at that time comprised two standard 'Weymouth-style' bow-windowed terraced houses at the end of Bank Buildings. It was not until the 1850s that this imposing façade was added. Two adjoining Georgian terrace houses were demolished in the late 1920s when the extension, shown here, was added to the chapel.

At No. 1 Augusta Place is the Bay View Hotel, its name unchanged since this 1958 photograph. The adjacent building is now holiday flats. It is likely that these two were once a single late-eighteenth century house. The extra storey on No. 1 is a prominent later addition. The Fairhaven Hotel at No. 3 is of the same period and it too has an additional storey, in the same style. Nos. 1–3 Augusta Place have been renumbered as 35–37 The Esplanade.

The Esplanade photographs on this and the following page illustrate the changes that one terrace – Chesterfield Place – underwent in the latter half of the twentieth century. Chesterfield Place comprises the buildings from the far left of the photograph to the Seacroft Hotel. The first, occupied by Marks & Spencer, was taken down in the 1960s when the store was enlarged and modernised. The next house was a dental practice in 1955 but it and the adjoining Trocadero ice cream parlour were both to be rebuilt by Barclays Bank when it extended through to the Esplanade from St Mary Street.

On the left, Marks & Spencer demolished the upper floors, adding a single additional storey to match the rest of the store's seafront façade. The abutting building on the right was later rebuilt by Barclays Bank.

Demolition of the upper floors in progress at Marks & Spencer.

This was the former Trocadero in 1959, rebuilt for use as Barclays Bank; conversion of the adjacent house (left) by Barclays followed later. The Seacroft Hotel today has remained almost unchanged since these 1950s' photographs were taken.

Weymouth's pretty cast-iron and glass Esplanade shelters were added to the seafront in the 1880s. Then, each one had a small balcony which overlooked the sands, but most of these balconies were lost in the first half of the twentieth century when the Esplanade was widened on the seaward side. The bigger shelter, just visible in the centre of the photograph, was a much later construction, erected in the 1930s.

Looking south along the Esplanade in July 1954. Three months earlier, fire had destroyed the Ritz Theatre, although at first glance, since the entrance and towers are still standing, it is difficult to appreciate that flames had totally devastated the auditorium and stage behind. Local firemen were disheartened by the news that the building they had fought so hard to save was to be totally demolished. The present Pavilion Theatre replaced it in 1960.

A superb fifties' view of Weymouth Esplanade. The big 1930s' seafront shelter in the foreground was then exposed to wind and rain. It has since been modified with glass partitions and seating. In the centre of the photograph the wide extension to the 'prom' around the Jubilee Clock is clearly visible. When first unveiled to commemorate the 1887 Golden Jubilee of Queen Victoria, the clock stood on the beach. It has never moved; the Esplanade has been widened around it.

W.H. Smith arrived in the town in 1905. More than fifty years on, in 1958, the shop still retained its old fashioned 'bookshop' windows. Turf accountants Wheatley then occupied Statue House.

By 1965 W.H. Smith had installed plate glass and the Model Railway had taken over the ground floor of Statue House. King George III's statue was first painted in heraldic colours in 1949; the traffic island which surrounds the King was constructed in 1956.

One wonders what King George III would have thought of the annual summer invasion of tens of thousands of holidaymakers to 'his' seafront. Since this view of 1969 the pedestrian crossing has moved northwards and is now controlled by traffic lights.

Old habits die hard and the two pedestrians in the centre of this picture are making their way across the traffic lanes close to the old pedestrian crossing, instead of heading up the Esplanade to the traffic lights and safety. Both the Tourist Information Centre and the Tea Cabin on the Esplanade have been considerably enlarged since 1970.

Royal Terrace was built on the former gardens of King George III's summer home, Gloucester Lodge. The royal 'shrubbery' extended south along the seafront and also included the land on which Frederick Place stands today. King George last visited the town in 1805 and although his summer home was not sold off until 1821, some of its grounds were acquired earlier to accommodate the increasing number of visitors holidaying in fashionable Weymouth. Royal Terrace was begun in 1815. It originally comprised 18 houses but in the 1920s the junction of Westham Road (then known as Little George Street) and the Esplanade was proving too narrow for ever-increasing road traffic. No. 18 was demolished and No. 17, shown here, is now the last house of Royal Terrace. The vertical line of the newer brickwork is still clearly visible today. Beneath it were the Southern Electricity Board show-rooms from which the Electra Hotel took its name.

An attractive seafront view of the late 1960s, with the Pier Bandstand (demolished in 1986) but without the Esplanade subway (constructed in 1982).

The sands were packed, indicating that Thursday 14 August 1958 was a hot and sunny day. Actually reaching the beach was none too easy. There were no traffic lights or crossings in the vicinity of the Jubilee Clock and these pedestrians appear to be taking quite a few risks to achieve their destination. Six years earlier Weymouth Road Safety Committee had submitted a plan to lessen traffic dangers on the seafront. The proposal in 1952 was to construct a subway under Westham Road and St Thomas Street as far as St Mary Street, and from there to the Esplanade. Although the Second World War had ended seven years before, enemy attacks were still very much in mind as a secondary suggested use for the proposed subway was as a large-capacity air-raid shelter in time of war. As well as reducing accidents, it was

envisaged that the plan would release some of the seven policemen employed supervising the summer seafront traffic for other duties. It was to be another thirty years before Weymouth's seafront subway was built, taking a quite different and controversial route. The 1982 subway lessened the dangers of crossing King Street opposite the Jubilee Clock, but did not, as many hoped it would, provide direct access to the beach.

Thirty or so years ago and the sands are a mass of windbreaks, deckchairs and sun worshippers. A policeman was on duty on this August day to guide beach-goers across the busy Esplanade.

The 1950s were the heyday of the day-trippers who poured into Weymouth by coach. They all disembarked at Westham coach park alongside Radipole Lake, and made their way to the beach via Westham Road, where the shops did a fair trade in seaside rock, ice creams, fish and chips and 'Kiss Me Quick' hats. Around teatime the holidaymakers all headed back to the coach park for the journey home. As coach after coach turned onto the Esplanade from Westham Road, the seafront became not a little congested, with up to 200 or so coaches leaving on a busy day. Four can be seen on this pleasant summer evening in August 1959. The Jubilee Clock sets the time at 7.05pm.

Gales lashed the coast in January 1965, hurling shingle onto the Esplanade and causing the familiar problems of flooding around the harbour and closure of the Preston Beach Road until thousands of tons of pebbles had been shovelled away. It was bitterly cold, too. Elsewhere, 46 counties in England and Wales were under a blanket of snow.

A clear almost 'aerial' view of the northern end of Melcombe Regis. The photograph was taken from the tower of the soon-to-be demolished Christchurch in 1956. Facing the bay is the Georgian royal residence Gloucester Lodge, with its Victorian extension to the south. Behind the Lodge (later the Gloucester Hotel), the former royal yard and stable area can clearly be seen – Gloucester Mews. The Odeon cinema (now closed) was in part a conversion of the old royal stables. Adjacent to it is the 'working end' of Channon's Garage with petrol pumps and workshops. A way through led to the firm's car showroom on the seafront.

Long-established local motor dealer Channon's Morris show-rooms were right in the centre of Weymouth Esplanade, adjacent to the Royal Hotel, until late in the 1960s. This was where the cars for sale were displayed, the firm's petrol pumps and work-shops being at the rear of the building, in Gloucester Mews. The ground floor shown here is now occupied by amusements. In 1963 the Cecchetti Dance School held their classes on the first floor.

Outside Channon's Morris car showrooms on the Esplanade in 1955. HPR 624, a new Ford 8 could be won for a shilling (5p). Weymouth Rotary Club was fund-raising for an Old People's Centre, which opened as the Pilgrim House Day Centre in Hope Square, in 1962.

The seafront Royal Arcade was originally an ornate late-Victorian shopping arcade lined with small shops. By the 1950s its central passageway had been converted to an amusement arcade. On the right, Rossi's shopfront was surmounted by two splendid ice cream cones which apparently disappeared back to ship with some skylarking sailors in the 1960s.

Belvidere on Weymouth Esplanade – three of its elegant and unspoiled houses designed around 1820. Although the town's building boom slowed a little after King George III's final visit in 1805, the development of the Esplanade continued northwards, being completed around 1855. Tilley's Garage was on the corner of Victoria Street and Crescent Street.

What looks to be the ultimate in Esplanade traffic chaos is probably not as serious as it appears at first glance. The cars are on the roadway in front of Brunswick Terrace – a cul-de-sac with no exit at its northern end. Most are driverless and it would seem that the area was being used as a car park, the assumption presumably being that most would be at the seaside all day so double-parking was in order! Even so, the chap in the centre of the photograph has found himself in an unfortunate spot for wheel changing. This was August Bank Holiday week 1959.

The Pier Bandstand viewed from the spire of St John's Church in 1962. Over the years proposals had been put forward to provide a roof over the fair-weather building with its open deck but none went ahead. Today only the Esplanade section of the Bandstand remains, its façade extended since this photograph was taken. The pier section was demolished in 1986.

The Pier Bandstand in 1958, Ted Heath and Harry Hudson providing the music with their respective bands. The front of the bandstand was later extended slightly and renovations in the 1990s changed its appearance a little more. It must have been a hot and sunny day, the sands are packed yet many of the men are formally dressed in suits or heavy jackets – some are even sporting overcoats!

The Pier Bandstand after refurbishment and extension in the 1960s. Pullingers was a popular restaurant on the first floor.

Greenhill Garage in 1960, in the days when pedestrians walked on the pavement beneath the extended arms of the petrol pumps as vehicles filled up with fuel.

Weymouth's necklace of seafront lights and the neon garland around the Pier Bandstand were switched off on 31 August 1939 and remained so for the duration of the Second World War and beyond. It was April 1949 before the Esplanade was lit up again. This photograph, showing also the illuminations in Greenhill Gardens, dates from summer 1958.

A corner of the old Weymouth Railway Station yard in November 1956. Opposite, awaiting demolition, is Christchurch. Today the lady on her bicycle would be facing the shops and flats of Garnet Court. Builder E.G. Coleman was taking down the 1870s' church, as indicated by his lorry parked outside. The Queen's Hotel was rebuilt in the 1930s in anticipation of the planned reconstruction and extension of the train station. War delayed these works and they faltered again in the 1950s when only partly completed. It was 1986 before the present station replaced the dilapidated 1850s' Brunel structure.

Fenced off and colonised by grass and weeds, this was where Christchurch stood until early in 1957. Before Garnet Court was built, the site was used for car parking. A chaotic Park Street still had two-way traffic and parking on both sides! Gloucester Street Church, demolished in 1980, is a prominent landmark on many of these town photographs.

A view of the timber sheds in Park Street, August 1957, with Gloucester Street Congregational Church in the background. Builders Bird & Cox were at Nos 24 and 26 (on the right).

The railway lines of the now-disused Weymouth Harbour Tramway reveal that this is Commercial Road, at its junction with Gloucester Street. The big corner site was then occupied by Betts & Company's timber yard and joinery works. Builders' merchants UBM Dibben took over the corner in later years before it was given over to car parking. In 2002 a new health-centre complex opened here. The row of cottages still stands, completed by The Star public house at the junction of Gloucester Street and Park Street. Gloucester Street Congregational Church was demolished in 1980 and replaced by the apartments of 'George Thorne House', commemorating one of the town's first Nonconformist ministers. The photograph was taken in 1963.

Betts' timber yard.

Builders' merchants UBM Dibben erected this new building on the site in the 1980s, all of Betts & Company's old buildings having been demolished, as was the high stone wall which had surrounded the timber yard. The 2002 health-centre complex now fills this corner.

Betts & Company's huge timber sheds spanned the ground between Park Street and Commercial Road. The timber firm once used an inlet of the sea adjacent to Gloucester Street as a pond for curing timber, in the days when the backwater was tidal, prior to the construction of Westham Bridge in 1921. The sheds, viewed here from Commercial Road, were used for further curing and seasoning of the wood. All were demolished in the 1980s and the area is now used for car parking. The building on the far right of this photograph was the New Bridge Hotel; it still stands, awaiting conversion to residential use.

This unusual single-storey house is Turton Villa, in Turton Street. Its plaque claims a building date of 1771 but the villa does not appear on early maps. It was in 1771 that Doctor John Turton was appointed physician to the Queen's household (Queen Charlotte, wife of King George III). Although this was long before the royal family's visits to Weymouth between 1789 and 1805, Turton also became physician to King George III in 1797 so his surname is a likely source of the Turton Street name.

A new Southern National bus garage opened in 1956. Its predecessor on the same site in Edward Street was destroyed in an enemy 'hit and run' raid on 21 October 1940. A single German plane swept in and unleashed several high-explosive bombs on the Commercial Road/Edward Street area. Three men and two children were killed in the raid which destroyed some ten houses in the vicinity, as well as the bus garage and several buses. Adjacent to the new garage a sign on the side of a terraced house announced that this was the Albion Inn in Commercial Road, which continued in business until the 1970s.

An interior view of the new bus garage. The houses of Terminus Street and Terrace Street disappeared from the map as a result of the air raid and subsequent rebuilding.

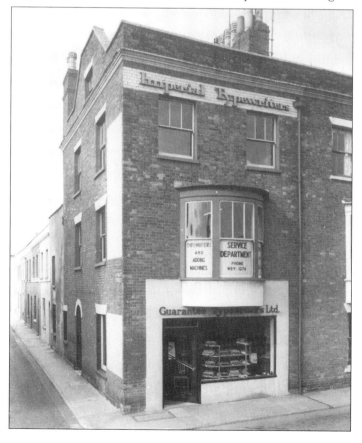

If the same proprietors were in business here today they would undoubtedly be selling computer equipment. In 1958 Guarantee Typewriters' shop was on the corner of King Street and Upway Street, a little thoroughfare which has not adopted the more familiar 'wey' ending to the place name.

Weymouth's Swannery car park in 1959. The bend in the road on the right-hand side of the picture no longer exists. It was the section of Radipole Park Drive which took traffic passing under the old railway viaduct along to the lakeside stretch of the road leading to Radipole. When the new road bridge (Swannery Bridge) was built in the late 1980s the section of Park Drive between Westham Bridge and the new bridge was closed to traffic. Vehicles now join Radipole Park Drive from the King Street roundabout.

Leading Ford dealers Crabb & Co. had their showroom and workshops in Crescent Street; this building, its ground floor much altered, is now a bingo hall. In the street outside, a line-up of 1950s Ford cars – Popular, Prefect, Consul and Zephyr.

Inside the showroom, prospective purchasers view the latest Ford Prefect in October 1956.

Sadly, a damaged negative of Tilleys the County Garage on the corner of Victoria Street and Crescent Street. It was replaced by the apartments of Nightingale Court. The empty ground on the left is now the site of Crescent Street Surgery.

A view that no longer exists, this was the large cleared site formerly occupied by Tilleys the County Garage, photographed in 1983.

One of several 'aerial' views of 1962, which Graham Herbert photographed when St John's Church spire was scaffolded for repair work. This shot moves north from the terraced streets of the Park District and into the wider streets and avenues of large properties around the church. In the foreground is Grange Road. Avenue Road turns round to the left and Cassiobury Road heads towards Radipole Lake. Across the water can be seen the then new developments at Southill.

Built as student accommodation at Weymouth Teacher Training College and designated 'Maiden Castle', this hostel opened in 1957 and was intended to house the whole and mainly female student body on the campus, rather than in lodgings around the town. The trainee teachers had been on the Dorchester Road site since 1946, taking over the Victorian buildings formerly occupied by the boys of Weymouth College, a public school which closed shortly after the outbreak of the Second World War, its students transferring to Wellingborough.

Westerhall's Hotel for the Royal Navy later became the Province of Natal Hotel and now has a large conservatory added at its northern end. The Lupins next door was also a hotel in 1965 but has since become a business centre.

North of the town Victorian and Edwardian mansions were built along Greenhill in the 1890s and early 1900s. This is Ingleton on the corner of Westerhall and Greenhill. Next to it the house formerly used as the Eye Infirmary is now the Trimar Hospice.

Two holiday coaches roll homewards in this view of Greenhill in July 1958. Large houses in the background were at the entrance to Melcombe Avenue and have been replaced by the apartment blocks of Beach Court and Greenhill Court. Rowland Court with surrounding grounds has also been built at Greenhill. The leading coach is a Maudslay.

A very basic Lodmoor Service Station on Preston Beach Road in the 1950s when service stations confined their sales to petrol and oil! The stone façade concealed the utilitarian hut-style building which was behind it. The service station's successor was demolished in 2000 and a skate park on the site has joined other leisure facilities on this area of Lodmoor. In the background, the hill on the right is today covered with houses as far as the hedge in the centre of the photograph.

A good view of the old Preston Beach Road wall in 1964 as a Mini-Paver lays new tarmac on the walkway. The diesel roller on the right of the photograph is an Aveling-Barford. Apartment blocks have replaced houses in the right background.

Lodmoor car park in 1957 – then a fenced-off square of infilled land which opened directly onto Greenhill – the van shown is turning into the entrance opposite the back gardens of the houses along Greenhill.

Nine years later and the Lodmoor car-park site has been extended and developed, its widened and land-scaped entrance still opposite No. 54 Greenhill. Marquees were erected to house stands at the Dorset Trades & Industries Exhibition of 1966, advertised as the biggest ever on the south coast. Among the attractions were guest appearances by comic actor Sid James and Philip Harben, one of TV's original 'celebrity chefs', plus a chance to see the Thunderbird stunt car from the James Bond 'Goldfinger' film. Today this entrance leads to The Lodmoor hotel/public house.

CHAPTER THREE
⪻ HARBOURSIDE ⪼
NORTH
Melcombe Regis

Weymouth's commercial pier was requisitioned by the War Department in the spring of 1940, followed by the cargo stage, and the Weymouth Harbour Tramway was restricted to use by the military until the autumn of 1945. The entire harbourside area between the Town Bridge and the pier had been in need of repair and modernisation before war broke out and a further six years of military use necessitated major reconstruction work in the late 1940s. Between 1948 and 1952 the lives of those occupying properties along Custom House Quay were totally disrupted as work progressed on widening the quay and constructing a new quay wall, building a new cargo stage and relaying the railway lines of the Harbour Tramway. Graham Herbert's photographs illustrate the scale of these operations in 1951 and 1952.

December 1951. The spot where the new quay walling joined the GWR's 1938 wall can clearly be seen opposite the end of Lower St Mary Street. The railway lines of the Weymouth Harbour Tramway were temporarily slewed while work went on and were later relaid. Cosens' paddle steamer *Consul* is in the foreground. Recent works have raised the height of this section of the wall along Custom House Quay.

By March 1952 work was well in hand on the new rail track. Motorcycles in the foreground belonged to Pankhurst's Motor Cycle showrooms which occupied the old Palladium cinema building on the Town Bridge (now the Rendezvous Club).

A month later the new road surface was being laid.

By mid-June 1952 this section of the work was almost complete. The paddle steamer at Trinity Quay is the *Empress*. Salvage contractor Louis Basso's tug *Scout* lies alongside Custom House Quay.

In scenes a little further along Custom House Quay, the Custom House and adjacent buildings overlooked the noise and dirt of the reconstruction work for four years. This series of views well illustrates the drabness of the immediate post-war years, showing doors and window frames badly in need of a coat of paint. Adjacent to the bow-windowed Custom House were the premises of Samways (coal merchant and haulage contractor) and the local Headquarters of the National Union of Seamen. Transformed today, this block is now the popular Sea Cow Restaurant.

Two months later there were signs of a return to normality. Kerbstones indicate the imminent provision of proper pavements outside the Custom House Quay properties, and the railway lines have advanced considerably.

The same spot, April 1952. In an age when health-and-safety considerations were less exacting than those of today, life at the harbourside continued much as usual. Custom House Quay was open to all who ventured along it to inspect the new works.

This was the roadway excavated outside the Fish Market prior to relaying the lines of the Weymouth Harbour Tramway in January 1952. The vessel lying in the cove is the *St Julien*.

The same scene three weeks later.

By April 1952 the Weymouth Harbour Tramway lines were relaid and the temporary track close to the harbour wall had been removed. The Fish Market (left) was built in 1855. In Victorian steamship days the constant humping of coal at the harbourside caused its catches to become grey, gritty and unsaleable. For much of the twentieth century the building was used to store fertiliser but now restored, it is once again being used for its original purpose of selling fresh fish.

The scene at the Custom House Quay/South Parade junction in December 1951. Rails for new cranes are being laid on the reconstructed cargo stage. The *St Julien* lies alongside; in the background is the Ritz Theatre, lost to fire in 1954. Allways is now the office of the Weymouth harbourmaster. Next to it, the bow-windowed house (which in the midst of all this upheaval still managed to retain a shrub or two outside its front door) is of the early nineteenth century. It is thought to have been the home of artist John William Upham (died 1829), painter of many Weymouth views including several of the harbour.

Closer to the pier in December 1951. Bicycles are leaning against offices then occupied by the Corporation harbourmaster and the port officer of the National Dock Labour Board. The tall building has now been converted to apartments. Dating from the early nineteenth century, it was a bank in its early years (giving its name to Bank Buildings). Considerably altered and extended, it later became the Marine Hotel, then the Edward Hotel.

Two final views of the 1950s reconstruction of Custom House Quay and the new cargo stage. April 1952 – awaiting road surfacing. In the background the little spire belonged to Holy Trinity School, Chapelhay. Badly damaged in Second World War air raids, the school buildings were demolished in 1961.

By this photograph of 16 June 1952 the work is complete. The cross-Channel steamship is the *St Helier*.

A special photograph of a special ship. When the paddle steamer *Empress* was due to be broken up in 1955, Graham Herbert photographed her engines. They were unique, the last set of oscillating engines still at work in a seagoing vessel. A Victorian design dating back to the 1850s, this set was installed in *Empress* when she was built in 1879. With the oscillating engine the piston rods were connected directly to the crankshaft, the necessary movement being created by the cylinders rocking to and fro on hollow bearings that admitted steam to the pistons. Fortunately, today these engines are preserved for all to see in the Southampton Maritime Museum.

Pretty girls, smooth guy, fast car… and what else would such a supercool group drink but – milk! Weymouth in 1957 was the setting for an advertising campaign by the Milk Marketing Board. It is an attractive harbourside scene, but it is the background which provides a snapshot of the port trade of forty-five years ago. The cargo vessel at the quay is the GWR's *Roebuck* and the trolleys are laden with her cargo of hundreds of chips of Guernsey tomatoes, a familiar sight until the mid-sixties when competition from other ports and a huge increase in the use of air freight services led to a dramatic decline in imports from the Channel Islands.

The Guernsey tomatoes (the cargo boats could bring in up to 30,000 'chips' (or baskets) in one consignment) were distributed all over the country in a season which lasted from mid-April until September/October. In the fifties, potatoes and other vegetables, salad items and flowers were also regularly brought in from the Channel Islands.

The final journey. Cosens & Company's paddle steamer *Emperor of India* left Weymouth for a Belgian breaker's yard in January 1957. She had made her last sailing (out of Bournemouth) in September 1956. It had not been a good season for the paddle steamer fleet and the *Emperor of India*, the most costly of the paddlers to maintain and repair, was selected for scrapping. The ship was built in 1906 and joined Cosens in 1908.

As the big paddler, almost fifty years old, was on her way out of the harbour to be broken up, she would pass the head offices of the company which owned her – Cosens, at 10 Custom House Quay. In 1962 economies necessitated the sale of this building and Cosens then concentrated all their activities at the engineering works in Commercial Road. Rebuilt in the late 1960s, these buildings too were vacated in 1987 when Cosens relocated to Portland.

A view of the run-down but once very fine Georgian harbourside warehouse on Custom House Quay early in 1958; it was to be demolished at the end of the year. The yacht *Rhona* is in the foreground.

As this book was being compiled, the scene at Custom House Quay changed dramatically. Early on the morning of 17 January 2002, fire devastated Maiden Street Methodist Church and the building is now a shell, its outer walls partially demolished for safety reasons. On the quayside in this 1957 scene the low building with a double roof line is the Fish Market of 1855, used for many years in the twentieth century as a store for bulk fertiliser. Happily today it has reverted to its original purpose and is now occupied by 'Weyfish'.

A poignant photograph, for this was Maiden Street Methodist Church in May 1955, when the church reopened following extensive refurbishment and modernisation. In January 2002, shortly after another renovation had been completed, fire raged through the church and the fine vista it provided at the end of St Edmund Street since 1867 is no more. Only the church's outer walls survive and a decision is awaited regarding its future.

The reopening of the church in 1955.

A further view of the modernised church in 1955. Extensive remodelling of the heavy decor of the Victorian interior included the removal of an ornate dark oak rostrum out of which the new pulpit and lectern shown in the previous photograph were made. The fine organ was also restored in 1955.

An attractive harbour shot of 1970 looking towards Melcombe Regis. On the far left, its rose window just visible, is Maiden Street Methodist Church, lost to fire in 2002. Along Custom House Quay the Sea Cow Restaurant had yet to expand into the two adjacent buildings it now occupies. John Deheer's had closed as had Cosens next door. The former offices of the shipping and engineering company were being used for storage, their former owner's name heavily obliterated. The pretty building with arched windows, formerly a Sailors' Bethel, was then home to Weymouth Youth Club, later becoming the Spinnaker Restaurant and currently the headquarters of the Royal Dorset Yacht Club.

This was the Inner Harbour slipway in Commercial Road in 1958, the scene considerably altered today following the construction of a new slipway and the redevelopment by the Borough Council of this formerly industrial area into a very pleasant harbourside walk. The final flats of the Chapelhay Heights development are nearing completion in the background.

A section of Commercial Road which is prone to flooding, as can be seen in this 1957 photograph of Webb Major's yard. The multi-storey car park stands here now.

The Nothe has always provided an ideal vantage point to both view and photograph vessels entering or departing the harbour. In this view the trees lining the footpath leading to the old Stone Pier have been used to good effect in framing one of the cross-Channel steamers, either *St Julien* or *St Helier*. Photographed between 1928 and 1937, the pre-war yachts and in particular the steam yacht in the foreground add to this delightful maritime scene.

St Julien and *St Helier* were Weymouth-based from 1925 until 1960, both serving with distinction during the Second World War, and are regarded as the two of the finest cross-Channel steamers ever to have operated out of Weymouth.

The *Roebuck* and her sister ship *Sambur* were the only GWR steamers built specially for cargo traffic, although each also had accommodation for 12 passengers. They entered service at Weymouth in 1925 and this photograph of the *Roebuck* is possibly pre-war. Both vessels did long service in the port, not leaving until the 1960s. *Roebuck* was broken up in 1965 – but look out for her when 'The Heroes of Telemark' is shown as a TV film repeat. Kirk Douglas was not the only star – filming of some of the war film's scenes took place in Dorset waters, with the *Roebuck* disguised to look like a Norwegian merchantman.

The old and the new. Another favourite 'Weymouth from the Nothe' view shows (foreground) the Cosens steamer *Consul* on the company's slipway in the spring of 1961. Coming to the end of her time in the port, *Consul*, built in 1896, was then the oldest paddle steamer still in service. The latest state-of-the-art passenger ferry *Ceasarea* was to be joined by her sister ship *Sarnia* for their first season in the Channel Islands service. The two 4000-ton vessels would be replaced by car ferries in the 1970s.

Although much of the harbour trade suffered from the effects of the Second World War, timber ships were still regular visitors to the port. The vessel being unloaded here in 1960 was the *Jytte Bres*.

Cargoes leaving Weymouth for the Channel Islands were varied. This lorry was being craned aboard in 1960. Across the harbour can be seen the now-demolished Cosens workshops and slipway on Nothe Parade.

A Class 3 diesel shunter takes the boat train and its passengers from the Channel Islands along Custom House Quay en route for Weymouth Railway Station. Weymouth is the only place in England where a main-line train travelled for a mile along a public highway. The Custom House on the left of the picture is now the local coastguard headquarters. John Deheer's warehouse closed in 1965, largely as a result of a drop in timber and fertiliser imports and is now a maritime-themed quayside attraction – the Deep Sea Adventure.

The first vessel to operate on Sealink's car ferry service to the Channel Islands in 1973 was the 1947 veteran *Falaise*, a converted former passenger ferry. She was nearing the end of her career and the following year, having suffered serious engine trouble, she was withdrawn from service, BR replacing her in August 1974 by a charter vessel, the Swedish *Svea Drott*. *Falaise*, twenty-seven years old, went to the breaker's at the end of 1974.

The fortunes of the local paddle steamer operators Cosens & Company were declining in the 1960s – their last paddler *Embassy* was to leave Weymouth for the breaker's yard in 1967. The company began concentrating its efforts on the general engineering and ship repairing aspects of its business. In 1965 work was completed on this 31m (104ft) landing stage for use at Cowes by the Southampton–Cowes ferry service. Here, the landing stage, seven steel tanks welded together, is about to be guided under the Town Bridge before being taken in tow for the Isle of Wight by the tug *Calshot*.

The jetty at Commercial Road, just prior to its departure in October 1965. In the background the paddle steamer *Princess Elizabeth* was laid up for the winter – she never sailed out of Weymouth again on pleasure trips. Sold in 1966, she is now used as a conference centre in France.

On Commercial Road in 1962 (opposite the back of today's Debenhams store) was the petroleum depot of the Esso Company. Small tankers came up harbour and offloaded their fuel here, for distribution by road to garages in the Weymouth area. The site is now used for car parking. All change along the far shore of the Backwater, too: (from left along Westwey Road) the electricity power station has been replaced by housing; the St John Ambulance Headquarters has been rebuilt (the original was found to be structurally unsafe); the pair of semi-detached houses made way for the Weston Probation Hostel; and when the Ambulance Station closed it was replaced by a motorcycle showroom.

Paddle steamers came up the Inner Harbour to refuel at the Esso Petroleum depot on Commercial Road. Here the *Princess Elizabeth* takes on fuel. The paddle steamer operated out of Weymouth in 1963, 1964 and 1965. All the background buildings shown along Commercial Road as far as the Arts Centre have since been demolished.

The sultry day that was 18 July 1955 in Weymouth was punctuated by lightning flashes and threatening rumbles of thunder. Heavy rain which started in the afternoon had become a deluge by evening. At nearby Martinstown 28cms (11 inches) of rain were recorded, the greatest ever known in the British Isles in a twenty-four-hour period. The River Wey rose dramatically, overflowing and flooding the villages along its course until the swollen waters surged into Radipole Lake. Here, beside Westham Bridge, lake, roadway and Melcombe Regis Gardens have become one vast expanse of water.

The sign at the entrance to Gloucester Mews car park offered very good advice in July 1955!

Radipole Park Drive disappeared completely when Radipole Lake overflowed above Westham Bridge. Some idea of the depth of the water can be gained from what can be seen of the lamppost (left). Melcombe Regis Gardens, Commercial Road and much of the Park District were also under water.

Anyone for tennis? Not on the courts at Melcombe Regis Gardens in July 1955! The tennis courts are no more – this area is now a car park.

CHAPTER FOUR
↫ HARBOURSIDE ↬ SOUTH

Weymouth and the Westham Shore

A harbour view little changed in forty-plus years, although there would be no buff funnels of Cosens' paddle steamers visible in the background today, and the tallest building across the harbour, Maiden Street Methodist Church, has gone, destroyed by fire in 2002. The imposing house on the right was built for a seventeenth-century merchant and mayor of Weymouth. As Weymouth's popularity as a health and pleasure resort grew in the eighteenth century, the house became the Assembly Rooms before visitors flocked to the opposite, more fashionable, side of the town. Known since then as the 'Old' Rooms, in the 1950s it was used by E.J.A. Cotton & Son, long-established local undertakers.

Another 'drink more milk' publicity shot from 1957, with a Co-op milk float at the harbourside. In the cove is the Air Ministry vessel *Rafmoor*, an 1880s craft with an interesting history. Originally named the *Albert Edward* she began life as a Red Funnel Line tug at Southampton. Renamed *Joy Bell III* and converted for passenger use she plied between the Channel Islands, fleeing before the German occupation in 1940. Post-war the Air Ministry took her over, renaming her yet again and as *Rafmoor* she arrived in Weymouth in June 1952. Used for a variety of jobs – towing RAF targets, placing marker buoys and assisting in the salvage of ditched aircraft – *Rafmoor* remained here until 1961, when, at seventy-five years old, she went to the breaker's yard.

An attractive harbour view from 1970. The vessel at the cargo stage is the *Elk*. On the right-hand side of the photograph can be seen the pleasure boat *Weymouth Belle*, formerly the *Bournemouth Belle*. She arrived here at the end of May 1967, just a few days before Weymouth's last paddle steamer, *Embassy*, departed for the breaker's yard. Operated by R.H. Wills & Son, the *Weymouth Belle* ran trips round the Bay, Portland Harbour and to Lulworth Cove. Sold in the mid-1970s, the *Weymouth Belle* (renamed *Souters Lass*) is still in service in Scotland.

Although Weymouth was to lose its fine Tudor house, No. 4 North Quay, strenuous efforts by national and local groups did save Nos 2 and 3 Trinity Street from demolition. The trust formed for the preservation of the houses had actually issued an order for a builder to commence repairs on 2 September 1939, the day before war was declared, so the planned restoration was immediately abandoned. The sixteenth-century houses then suffered some Second World War bomb damage and are seen here in their dilapidated post-war state in 1958. Weymouth Civic Society and local architect Ernest Wamsley Lewis restored Nos 2 and 3 superbly and they are now an attraction, open to the public at specified times.

The Tudor cottages, restored.

High above the harbour, with superb views from first-floor bow windows are the early-nineteenth-century houses of Trinity Terrace, fortunately spared the Second World War bombs which destroyed so much of Chapelhay. This scene is from May 1958.

Cosens' paddle steamer *Consul* at Trinity Quay, her customary Weymouth Harbour berth, in 1962. Sadly this was the last decade of the company's paddle steamers in the port. *Consul* was losing money and was sold in March the following year, returning to Weymouth in the service of another company and running mainly to Lulworth Cove. She returned to Devon, her county of origin in 1964 (reverting to her original name *Duke of Devonshire*) and was broken up in 1968.

The Phoenix Stores, fruit and vegetable merchants, occupied this impressive old warehouse building on North Quay and its high walls provided splendid advertising space. Sharing the building were the Phoenix Works, operated by marine salvage contractor Louis Basso. The building took its name from a previous occupant, the Phoenix Aerated Water Company. Spared a little longer than most of the North Quay buildings, the Phoenix premises and adjacent garage were reduced to rubble in 1965.

North Quay with, sadly, No. 4, the historic Tudor house (centre) partially demolished. An oak staircase, in remarkably fine condition considering the building's derelict state prior to clearance, was taken out and used in St Ann's Church at Radipole. A few days after this photograph was taken on 12 August 1961 the old house had a blazing swan-song when timber and rubble smouldering in its shell burst into flames, threatening the neighbouring (then still functioning) Town Bridge Garage.

This view a little further along North Quay brings us to the North Quay Café, adjoining the historic Tudor house, razed in 1961. The garage and tall Phoenix Stores building lasted until 1965. Chapelhay Heights in the background were built to replace the blitzed streets above the harbour. Another air-raid casualty was Holy Trinity School (top left) bombed on 17 November 1940. The children were temporarily housed in other buildings in the town until their new school opened in Cross Road in 1952. The Victorian school building was demolished in 1961 and Trinity Court housing now fills the site.

A hint of things to come. Close inspection of these houses on North Quay in the late 1950s reveals that some are boarded up and demolition would follow in 1961. Here today stand the town's Municipal Offices and car parks. The baker's roundsman is delivering his loaves by bicycle, complete with giant wicker basket on its front carrier.

An attractive and nostalgic view of North Quay in the 1950s.

Land Rovers were designed to tackle a wide range of duties. This one, in 1957, was the Land Rover Fire Engine. The vehicle was particularly designed for use at fires in rural and forestry areas. Being demonstrated at Weymouth Fire Station on North Quay, the twin full-size hoses delivered water at 210 gallons per minute and sent it 22m (75ft) up the hose-drying tower in the station yard.

Two small cottages which enjoyed fine views of the harbour and town before their demise in November 1965. These were Nos 31 and 32 Chapelhay Street and the front steps shown in the photograph can still be found on the edge of the street.

A 1958 view of North Quay – behind the Neptune soft drinks store can be seen the backs of Nos 31 and 32 Chapelhay Street – the cottages in the previous photograph. Tarps Randall is at the helm of the fishing boat *Silver Dawn* carvel-built by James & Caddy in the 1950s. In the background (left) can be seen White Motor Boats *My Girl* and *Endeavour* which then operated Portland Harbour trips from alongside the Pier Bandstand. Today these two still make trips to Portland, operating now from the Cove.

Pre-war vintage photographs of Chapelhay and High Street seem to be few and far between. It is a great shame that most views of the once lively and thriving community that was High Street show its buildings in their derelict and dilapidated post-war state, as here, looking up towards Boot Hill. The boarded-up pub on the left was the Weymouth Arms.

Such a scene of dereliction in High Street! This 1959 view looks up towards the Old Town Hall. No. 10, Oliver the fish merchant is on the left. Beyond Oliver's, before the Second World War, flourished the businesses of Louis Basso, salvage contractor; Henry Randall, boat proprietor; Horlock's fried fish shop, and fruiterer Mockridge. Some continued in business among the boarded-up properties after the war but all made way for the redevelopment of North Quay in the 1960s.

The north side of High Street in the 1950s, the buildings almost back to back with those along North Quay. The Phoenix Stores are on the far right. An abundance of buddleia is growing in every crack and crevice of the abandoned properties.

A face-on view of the warehouse building seen in the previous photograph. Possibly No. 55 High Street, its use prior to the Second World War is a little uncertain, although it may have been a sawmill at some stage.

The heart of Chapelhay was ripped out during Second World War air raids in 1940 and 1941. Post-war plans for the area's redevelopment were slow to produce results and there was much pressure to speed up the rebuilding of these shattered streets. This photograph of 1957 shows properties in Franchise Street awaiting clearance. They would be replaced by flats – Chapelhay Heights. Some completed blocks can be seen in the background. The view is taken looking down the street from the Boot Hill end – and the house on the left, No. 82, still stands.

Seen from the other direction – the bomb-damaged and boarded-up former shops of tobacconist and confectioner A. Holgate and A.A. Skillman, the shop's fascia board advertising its proprietor as 'electrical engineer', although this was also a general store for the Chapelhay district.

It was the mid-1950s before protracted discussion on the redevelopment of bomb-ravaged Chapelhay finally produced results. As new flats went up to replace the old streets of terraced houses, a shopping precinct was laid out to serve the 'new' community. First to open in March 1957 at No. 1 Gordon Row was the Co-op, fittingly since their Chapelhay shop had been an air-raid casualty in 1941. Note the headscarf worn by the lady second from right – its portrait of Queen Elizabeth II identifies it as a 1953 Coronation souvenir!

The completed precinct, Gordon Row, in 1959. The Co-op is on the right.

Chapelhay, the worst-hit area of Weymouth during the air raids of the Second World War, was rebuilt in the 1950s. Blocks of flats and rows of shops went up and in 1959 the community's new 'local' opened in Franchise Street, to replace the bombed 'General Gordon' of pre-war years. The Prospect was the first post-war pub built by Hope Square brewer John Groves. Facilities included a skittle alley and its first landlord Mr Robert Stanley declared firmly that there would be 'no telly', his view being that TV was a conversation-killer and had no place in a traditional English pub.

The new pub's attractive nautical sign. When first planned it was to be called The Hawk, but the final choice is much more fitting, celebrating the superb views from Chapelhay of Weymouth Harbour and also recalling those properties in Prospect Place which were demolished after the Second World War – these included another 'local', The Rising Sun.

Springfield House stood at the top of Boot Hill. Glance right as you pass the St Leonard's Road turning on Rodwell Road and you will see the gate pillars of the old house, built for the Devenish brewing family. Its last owner, Major J.H.C. Devenish, died in 1953. His family home was, like many other large houses, requisitioned during the Second World War and also suffered air-raid damage. Unable to return to it, the Major spent his final years at the Old Castle Hotel, Rodwell. Springfield was demolished, having proved too costly to convert to 'homes for the widows of officers of the Army, Navy and Air Force and of the Clergy', as the Devenish family had wished. Smaller units were built for the purpose in various parts of the borough and in the former grounds of Springfield House.

This prefab building opened in February 1955 as the new headquarters of the 9th Weymouth (Holy Trinity) Scout Group. It stood in the grounds of the Sidney Hall, entered via the gate in Weston Road. Weymouth Football Ground is visible beyond the hut. All the buildings shown were cleared in the 1980s to make way for a supermarket (now Asda) and its car parks. At the same time the 'Rec' relocated to Southill.

Great changes have taken place along the Backwater's western shore since the 1950s. From this once major industrial site have been cleared the redundant buildings of the local gasworks, electricity power station and sewage works, although the gasometer on Westwey Road, under construction in this 1956 view, remains today. Close to Westham Bridge, in a supposedly 'temporary' single-storey prefab, was Weymouth's first public library, which opened in 1948 and lasted until 1990 when the present Weymouth Library opened in the town centre. Its site was used as a car park for ten years until work began on construction of the Harbour View apartments, a site which includes the now-demolished Health Centre of 1930 on the far right.

A second photograph from 1958. Sport and industry (football ground and gasworks) have today been replaced by shopping, benefits and justice (Asda, DSS and the Magistrates Court) on Westwey Road. Taking WH50 *Silver Dawn* out of the harbour is Tarps Randall.

Up goes the present gasometer on Westwey Road in the late 1950s, in fact not long before gas ceased to be produced in Weymouth on 1 November 1958. The paddle steamer in the background is the *Emperor of India*. Although the gasometer is currently in use, its site is scheduled for future redevelopment.

An unusual shot of Westwey Road taken from the Inner Harbour. Great changes in the background scene have taken place since 1975. The Sidney Hall, adjacent 'small' Sidney Hall and other buildings on the site were cleared in the 1980s to make way for a supermarket development and necessary large car parking area. On the right, the austere office block Westwey House of the 1970s has been enlarged and remodelled and is practically unrecognisable today.

Westwey House, before the alterations of the 1990s, is on the left. The girder framework in the course of erection next to it is for the Magistrates Court, opened in 1978. The gasholder in the centre of the photograph and most of the other Weymouth Gasworks buildings have been cleared, apart from the one remaining gasometer on Westwey Road (right).

Weymouth's sewage pumping station was once housed in these now-demolished buildings in the corporation yard at the end of Westwey Road. Older photographs show two tall chimneys on the Backwater's western shore – one belonged to the electricity generating station, the second was part of these works.

A walk along here today would be a hazardous undertaking. Since its construction in the late 1980s, Weymouth Way, part of the relief road scheme, has taken traffic to and from Weymouth along this western shore of Radipole Lake. Nothing remains of the buildings in the background. On the far left Weymouth Grammar School opened at the end of Alma Road in 1913 as the Victoria Secondary Schools. These were in the 'old wing', a 'new wing' was added later. The school moved to new premises at Charlestown in the 1960s and Weymouth College (then South Dorset Technical College) took over the old Grammar School wings. The college had opened in 1939 in the purpose-built block on the right of the photograph – the 1970s building in the centre was also a college development. The whole lot, including the single-storey extensions on the far right, has been cleared and extensive housing development is under way on the site. Weymouth College now operates from a single extended site in Cranford Avenue.

In a building only recently demolished, woodwork students of the South Dorset Technical College demonstrate their skills in 1961. All the former College and Grammar School buildings along Newstead Road have been demolished and in 2002 the site is rapidly filling with new houses.

Stranded during the summer floods of 1955 were these coaches parked in Westham coach park which became an extension of Radipole Lake as the waters rose.

The two buses in the background of the previous photograph are also shown here, close to Westham Bridge where the sluices became choked and damaged by the great mat of reeds swept down from the upper reaches of the lake. If the bus on the right parked on this spot today it would be across the entrance to the pedestrian subway close to the busy roundabout leading to Weymouth Way and the Swannery Bridge.

North of the coach park, flood water, debris and a mass of reeds from the lake swirl around the sodden funfair.

Chipperfield's funfair occupied a lakeside site just north of the old railway viaduct.

CHAPTER FIVE
‹ꭗ VISITORS AND ꭗ›
LOCAL FOLK
Cup-winners, carnival queens and an all-star cast

Were you there? Saturday, 1 March 1952 was the final opportunity for most people to travel by train to Easton, Portland. The Weymouth and Portland Railway line officially closed to passengers the following day. These folk are waiting on the platform of Melcombe Regis Station, nothing of which remains today. The site is now filled by the apartments and grounds of Swannery Court in Commercial Road.

Guests at the Gloucester Hotel in December 1954 enjoyed this non-traditional Christmas cake, a finely detailed iced representation of the hotel itself, complete with verandah and Jubilee Clock outside.

This photograph labelled '25th Anniversary – Presentation' was taken at the Pier Bandstand and is a Radipole Steam Laundry staff gathering in 1955.

Outside Maiden Street Methodist Church on the occasion of the church's reopening following extensive refurbishment in 1955. The Minister, the Reverend John Charlton Blackburn is fourth from left, front row.

Chickerell Football Team, photographed in 1955. Only Charlie Oldridge (second from left, front row) still lives in the village. The trainer, Fred Plummer, is on the extreme right, back row.

Holy Trinity Church of England Infants' and Junior Schools moved into new premises in Cross Road in 1952, their Chapelhay building having received more than one visit by German bombers during the Second World War. The children were educated in various temporary classrooms until the new school was ready. Outside it in 1956 is the Junior School football team with teacher Mr David Lewis.

With their school building in the background this was Chickerell School's cup-winning Country Dance Team in 1959. Teachers are Mr Ken Maundrell and Mrs Audrey Hellier. Several of the group still live in the village.

The railway to Weymouth opened on 20 January 1857 and centenary celebrations were underway in 1957 when the appropriately decorated loco *Glasfryn Hall* awaited 'engine driver' Charlotte Wootton, Mayor of Weymouth who took the train the length of the platform. She was no doubt glad of the assistance of Driver Puckett (on the footplate, right) and Fireman Murphy. On the platform with the Mayor are Stationmaster W.E. Flew (left) and Guard W. G. Tucker. After the removal of flags and bunting the *Glasfryn Hall* left on the 9.35am Western Region daily service to Swindon.

Does the Mayor look a little apprehensive as the train prepares to leave? She was in safe hands – Driver Puckett and Fireman Murphy had driven Her Majesty the Queen from Yeovil to Dorchester four years earlier.

A splendid start to the centenary celebrations as the *Glasfryn Hall*, Mayor Wootton on the footplate, sets off.

When First Sea Lord the Earl Mountbatten was at sea off Portland in the new frigate HMS *Salisbury* in March 1957, Lady Edwina Mountbatten visited several organisations in the local area. As Superintendent-in-Chief of the Nursing Division of the St John Ambulance Brigade, she met more than a hundred people at the Brigade Headquarters in Westwey Road. Lady Mountbatten is seen here with Dr R.V.S. Cooper (of Weymouth), the St John County Commissioner, and (left) Mayor of Weymouth Charlotte Wootton. The St John Ambulance Brigade Hall, completed in 1939, was found to be structurally unsafe and was demolished in 1994. The present Brigade Headquarters in Westwey Road opened in 1995.

A packed Pier Bandstand audience watches one of the weekly heats in the annual 'Miss Weymouth' contest. Resident musicians were Harry Hudson and his Melody Men. Imagine the rush to get under those shelters along the sides of the open deck when it rained!

Weymouth's stunning bathing beauty queen in 1958 was Shirley Horton, seen here posing on the roof of one of the shelters which ran along the sides of the Pier Bandstand's deck.

The big retort houses of the gasworks on Westwey Road dominate many views of Weymouth Backwater's western shore. The two appear very similar but were built some years apart. The one on the left dates from the gasworks expansion of the early 1930s; its partner on the right was an addition in the 1950s. Gas ceased to be manufactured in Weymouth on 1 November 1958 (and proposals to develop the area for residential use were put forward as early as 1960). The retort houses were pulled down in 1962. The lorries and their drivers were entrants in the 1958 Lorry Driver of the Year competition.

A happy group photograph and a splendid cake for the fortieth birthday celebrations of Upwey and Broadwey Women's Institute in 1958. The WI Hall, now demolished, stood alongside Shepstone's Garage on Dorchester Road (now rebuilt as Wey Valley Motors). President Mrs Nora Boradaile Bell stands behind the cake. The banner, worked by WI members, hangs in their present meeting room at Upwey and Broadwey Memorial Hall. Several of the ladies pictured here are still WI members forty-four years on!

Local lasses, visitors or dancers from Charlie Drake's summer show at the Alexandra Gardens Theatre?
An Esplanade scene from 1958.

Two stylish young women having the attractions of Portland Navy Days 1958 pointed out to them are standing on the jetty alongside HMS *Pellew*. 'See the ships and meet the men' ran the adverts for the ever-popular three-day event which attracted thousands of visitors.

Duncan Sandys, Minister of Defence in Harold Macmillan's cabinet, visited Portland Naval Base in May 1958. Accompanied by the Deputy Chief of the Naval Staff and other Ministry of Defence officials, he spent six hours in talks with naval experts and watched demonstrations of submarine and anti-submarine tactics at sea. The party embarked on the submarine HMS *Truncheon* at Portland and were later transferred by helicopter to the frigate HMS *Grenville*.

The transfer to HMS *Grenville*. In the centre of the photograph is the frigate HMS *Dundas*.

Another reminder of the days when many naval vessels were to be seen in the waters around Weymouth. In post-war years the Royal Navy's Portland Training Squadron was established to train new-entry ratings. Shown here is one of the battleships based at Portland for this purpose, HMS *King George V.*

A Southern League victory for Weymouth in the match versus Tonbridge in October 1958 (score Weymouth 2 Tonbridge 0). Weymouth Football Club relocated to Southill when 'the Rec' shown here was sold for a supermarket development. The tree on the right of the picture was one of a number around the Sidney Hall; the big gas retort houses were on the site of Westwey House. Today, the players would be kicking around the Asda store!

Weymouth and South Dorset Arts Centre's 'Georgian Fair' was a popular summer event in July 1960. It was held in the grounds of Belfield House (built in King George III's reign) and stallholders and entertainers were appropriately costumed. 'King George III', mounted on a chestnut mare, rode in a procession preceded by Portland Town Band to Belfield, off Buxton Road. The house was open to visitors, there were stalls and sideshows, plus dancing and recreated Georgian sports and games to enliven the afternoon. And the sun shone!

Topping the bill of 'Let's Make a Night of It', Weymouth Pavilion's summer show in August 1960 were Eric Sykes and Hattie Jacques, starring with Cyril Stapleton and his Show Band in twice-nightly performances at 6 and 8.30pm. There was no shortage of live entertainment. The Alexandra Gardens Theatre also provided two shows each evening – the line-up here included Anne Shelton, Morecambe and Wise, Gladys Morgan and Daisy May with ventriloquist Saveen. If none of these appealed, there were daily 3pm and 7pm performances of 'Strike it Lucky – the big give-away show' at the Pier Bandstand. Eric Sykes is pictured here with three members of the Weymouth Operatic Society chorus.

A Weymouth Grammar School group photo from 1955. On the front row (centre) is Dr Hamilton. The superb gates, currently somewhat dilapidated, stand at the end of Holland Road and opened onto the school's 'new' wing. The Grammar School transferred to a new site at Charlestown is the mid-1960s. Occupancy of these buildings by the South Dorset Technical College (later renamed Weymouth College) followed, but they were demolished on the transfer of all the College departments to one site at Cranford Avenue in 2001. New homes are being built on the land behind the gates.

Weymouth Grammar School prefects of 1967, the photograph taken outside of one of the new buildings on the Charlestown site. Centre front the teachers are (from left): Mrs Mary Bawn, Headmaster Mr S.F. Parsons, Deputy Head Miss Kitty Kane and Mr H.H.C. 'Drasher' Hill. The Grammar School buildings are now part of Budmouth Technology Centre.

Members of the Weymouth-Louviers Twinning Association line up outside the old Municipal Offices in Clarence Buildings for a group photo: Weymouth's Mayor Mrs Iseult Legh is centre, and M. Vincelot, Mayor of Louviers fourth from right, front row. The official twinning ceremony took place at the Alexandra Gardens Theatre the following evening, 4 April 1959. This building, now converted to apartments, was offices for Weymouth and Melcombe Regis Borough Council from 1904 until 1971 when the North Quay building opened.

The choir of St Ann's Church, Radipole in May 1966. The front-row line-up includes (centre) the late Reverend Eric Allen, and (third from left) choirmaster Eric Ricketts, architect, local historian and author of the indispensable and delightfully illustrated four-volume work *The Buildings of Old Weymouth.*

Weymouth Operatic Society members pose for a group photograph on board the *Ceasarea* at Weymouth Quay in 1963.

These Vickers Armstrong bowlers in Melcombe Regis Gardens would find themselves in a very changed scene today. To the bowlers' right the tennis courts have been replaced by pay-and-display car parks. A car park also occupies the site behind them where the huge timber sheds stood in Commercial Road until the 1980s. The match was being played in July 1965.

An attractive 'rose walk' ran along the side of the tennis courts, as shown in this earlier view of 1958. Today's bowlers' view is of the road bridge which has spanned the water since 1989. The rail viaduct shown here was removed in the mid-1970s.

The first fund-raising carnival processions in Weymouth date back to the end of the nineteenth century and, interrupted only by war, the annual celebrations and procession have taken place each summer in the town. Weymouth's 1953 Coronation Year Regatta and Carnival Queen was Joyce Hunt seen here with her attendants Pat Garman, Christine Hawker, Audrey Brown and Heather Gale.

The 1953 Carnival saw the Dagenham Girl Pipers entertaining the crowds at the packed Pier Bandstand. In the background the Hotel Burdon is now the Prince Regent Hotel.

An extravaganza of floral decoration for the Carnival Queen's float in 1955. Sylvia Ford's attendants were Heather Gale and Jean Spencer. Since 1966 the procession has commenced its seafront route at Lodmoor car park but prior to this the assembly point was the Sidney Hall coach park at the end of Westwey Road. The floats made their way along North Quay, over the Town Bridge and up St Thomas Street to the Esplanade then Westerhall. Return route was from Greenhill along the promenade, round the Alexandra Gardens then back to the Sidney Hall via Westham Bridge and Westwey Road. Cosens' paddle steamer *Empress* is in the background of this photograph.

Typically irrepressible, diminutive comedian and summer show star Charlie Drake attempted to embrace the Regatta Queen Elizabeth White and both her attendants Daphne Dagger (left) and Pamela Wilcox (right) at the crowning ceremony in 1958.

There is barely room for the Carnival floats to make their way through the crowds on Weymouth Esplanade in August 1959. The very hot day brought with it an invasion of wasps and the St John Ambulance Brigade dealt with more than 50 casualties who had been stung. Here, the RNLI leads the way, followed by the Territorial Army's DUKW vehicle disguised as the Loch Ness Monster, which won the 920 Coy RASC unit a third prize. Surprise announcement of the day was that the following year's Regatta and Carnival would be combined – they were usually held on two separate days in August.

First-prize winner in the National Trade Vehicles class at the 1963 Carnival was local baker F. Wilkins' 'Sunblest' entry. The floats assembled on the coach park at the end of Westwey Road, opposite the Sidney Hall and adjacent to the gasworks. The gasometer (right) is still on Westwey Road, but its companion and the electricity-generating station chimney have gone.

A year later the Spar shop contingent lined up for a photograph, supplied with some impressive advertising material by Heinz 57 varieties. They duly scooped third prize in the Trade section, first prize going to the Britvic float in front.

Three traction engines brought up the rear of the 1966 Carnival procession, a popular finish to the parade as they progressed down the Esplanade with many shrill hoots and much letting-off of steam. First-prize winner YA 2481 towed the 'Bathing Belles' of the County Hospital's Social Club. Not far behind (and second-prize winner) is a Hayden Princess, also with a 'bathing' theme.

Just what's needed on Carnival Day – sun and crowds – making 1966 a memorable year.

A firework display traditionally rounds off Carnival Day fun.

The man standing at Priory Corner with surely one of the country's most stunning views behind him is Guy Barnett, South Dorset's first Labour MP. In a surprise 1962 by-election result he defeated Tory, Angus Maude, after Sir Piers Debenham split the Conservative vote by standing as an Anti-Common Market candidate. In 1964 Guy Barnett was on a vote-catching tour of the constituency prior to the General Election – but he was to lose the seat.

Jeannette Matthews shows Miss World the latest Marks & Spencer lingerie range.

Lesley Langley, of Preston, Weymouth was 'Miss World' in 1966, a double success for Dorset as Ann Sidney from Poole had held the title the previous year. Lesley's mother Mrs Doreen Orpen was employed by Marks & Spencer in St Mary Street and store manager Jim Shaw invited Miss World to visit Marks & Spencer in January 1966. Here she chats to the youngest member of staff, Wendy Farrell (now Wendy Webb and still with Marks & Spencer).

It was quite an occasion in August 1966 when Weymouth's Mayor, Lucie Hill, switched off the town's direct current electricity supply for ever as local consumers were all now using the alternating current supply. Weymouth Corporation was the last DC subscriber, having used it earlier in 1966 at the Stanley Street pumping station which cleared flood water from the town's low-lying areas. The big 'switch-off' took place at the SEB's Stavordale Road generating station. The Corporation had started supplying Weymouth's electricity in the early 1900s and continued until nationalisation in 1948. Mrs Hill is pictured with SEB's district manager Mr F.A. Hitchcock.

The show at the Pavilion Theatre for the 1968 season was 'Summer Spectacular'. Its star was popular comedian Tony Melody (centre stage), well known for his roles in radio's 'The Clitheroe Kid' as Mr Higginbottom, and TV's 'Coronation Street' in which he played Harold Eaton. Also on the bill was singer Nancy Whiskey, the original 'Freight Train' skiffle girl.

The present Redlands Sports Centre opened in 1974. Prior to this the ground was served by the pavilion shown here. In 1960 it had replaced the players' previous facility, a run-down Nissen hut.

A long-awaited leisure facility opened in Weymouth in 1974, the swimming pool in Knightsdale Road.

Graham Herbert was a keen Rotarian and his photograph of 7 July 1980 shows the Greenhill Gardens floral display commemorating the 75th anniversary of Rotary International. Local members gathered for the 'opening' ceremony by the Mayor of Weymouth and Portland, Mrs Joyce Litschi. She and her husband Fredy are seen here being greeted by Rotary Club president Mr E.J. Jones, former Town Clerk of Weymouth. In the background (right) is the Stainforth Memorial. It commemorates the success of Flight Lieutenant G.H. Stainforth in the Schneider Trophy Seaplane races of 1931 in which he achieved an average speed of 407.5 mph. Stainforth was an old boy of Weymouth College and the memorial originally stood in the College grounds when it was a boys' public school. The air ace was killed in action in 1942.

CHAPTER SIX

﹂◈ OUT OF TOWN ◈﹄

A little wander beyond

Attractive roadside signs welcoming holidaymakers to Weymouth reminded them of the town's maritime history and its Georgian seaside heritage. Put up on Preston Hill and Ridgeway in 1958, they were the work of a Bridport signwriter, Mr F.G. Biles. These days signs welcome visitors to the combined Borough of Weymouth and Portland.

Following the Second World War, 'Glenthorne', in Old Castle Road was converted for use as a British Legion Women's Convalescent Home. It had originally been built in the 1890s and is now once more a private house. Photographed in 1957.

The 'Kingswood' in Rodwell Road has been a hotel since the early 1930s. The building has been considerably extended since this 1964 photograph.

Two details of a block of four cottages built in 1829 for 'the Habitation of Four Poor Widows' of Weymouth. They stood at the junction of Wyke Road and Gypsy Lane; a view of the street scene can be found in *Weymouth: The Golden Years*, page 137. Funded by the 1716 Jonathan and Rebecca Edwards Charity, the tiny houses lasted until the late 1950s. They were replaced by modern bungalows in Rodwell Avenue.

The almshouses stood on the south or 'Weymouth' side of the harbour. The plaque on the building omits any reference to widows from Melcombe Regis benefiting from the charity, which intended the homes to be for widows from Holy Trinity Parish.

Graham Herbert lived at Faircross Avenue, Weymouth, in the 1960s and took this photograph of snow piled high along the street in the severe winter of 62/63. His house, No. 9, is on the right.

One of the coves between Sandsfoot and Ferrybridge, this little sandy bay with rock pools to explore, shrubby cliffs and a few beach chalets was a locals' delight. Developed as a windsurfing centre it changed beyond recognition and now that the surfers have moved to a base at Portland its buildings stand empty and abandoned, although thay may now become HQ for a local sailing club.

A second view of the Sandsfoot coastline, very little commercialised in 1967.

A view of the Downclose Estate at Wyke Regis, the photograph taken from the old Weymouth and Portland Railway line between Rylands Lane and Ferrybridge. The empty area in the centre of the picture was developed in the late 1990s. The houses of Douglas Road were built here, the street name continuing the tradition of Downclose Estate in beginning with 'D'.

Work began on the construction of a new secondary school at Wyke Regis in 1955. All Saints Church of England Modern School (now All Saints CE School) opened in 1958, the year after this photograph was taken. The school has been much enlarged since and extensions continue. The large house on the right was 'Stormont', a children's home in the thirties and forties. It was demolished to provide the site for the houses of Swaffield Gardens built here in 2000.

The school viewed from Buxton Road in 1957.

Residents of Dawlish Crescent at Wyke Regis had cause to recall not only the floods of July 1955 but also those of October that same year. Their houses (right) were overlooked by a large field which was being levelled to become a playing field for the new All Saints School. Two inches of rain fell on the night of 18/19 October 1955, filling up the 'dish' that the excavators had carved out. This overflowed, drains were unable to cope, and water and silt cascaded down into the back gardens at the top of the Crescent, flooding a number of properties.

A view of Portland Road in the mid-1960s, still a very recognisable scene apart from some changed business names. On the left, the 'Wyke Hotel' is now the Wyke Smugglers.

Much altered since 1958, this garage still stands on Portland Road, opposite the gardens at Wyke Regis. The showroom block on the right of the picture has been demolished, as has the house on the left (then No. 65 Portland Road) where the present garage displays its cars for sale.

On 7 April 1962, Mayor William Ward opened Weymouth's first purpose-built branch library at Wyke Regis, replacing a part-time service housed at the old Wyke Regis Junior School. In 1964 the library was joined on the Foord's Corner/Portland Road site by a new health centre and more recent extensions linked the two buildings under one roof. In the background of this photograph, taken as the library building neared completion, can be seen 'Stormont', the now-demolished house which was once a children's home.

This 1959 view of Ferrybridge was taken some twenty years before the structural faults which led to its replacement were discovered. Just visible beyond the road bridge is the second bridge which once crossed the water here, carrying the Weymouth and Portland Railway to the island. The rail bridge did not outlive its companion. The line to Portland finally closed in 1965 and the bridge was removed in 1971.

Ferrybridge in 1983, showing definite signs of the structural decay which was causing it to sag. Almost ninety years old, the iron bridge was rusting out. It had served Portland well and its designer, distinguished engineer Sir John Coode, could not have envisaged in the 1890s the amount of twentieth-century traffic which would pass over it, his being the age of the horse and carriage. The present, resited, Ferrybridge was completed in 1985.

Looking across from the old road bridge at Smallmouth to the former Whitehead Torpedo Works in 1975. During its hundred-year-plus history other company names appeared at the factory – Vickers, Wellworthy and A.E Pistons – but final closure of the engineering works was followed by the complete clearance of the site in 1997. The housing development which now fills it, Harbour Point, incorporates plaques detailing a little of the history of Whitehead's, which played a vital role in the development of 'new' Wyke along the Portland Road in the 1890s and early 1900s.

The business of W & J Tod Ltd of Ferrybridge, Wyke Regis closed in 2002. Founded in the early 1930s, the company pioneered glass-fibre boat building. The view, taken from The Fleet in 1961, shows Ferrybridge Cottages in the background.

Second World War air-raid damage can be clearly seen in this 1955 photograph of Shrubbery Lane, Wyke Regis. On the far right of the picture is Shrubbery Lodge. It and the neighbouring house still stand but the adjacent derelict property was to be demolished and completely rebuilt. Shrubbery Lane has since been realigned and Nos 16-18A now overlook a grassy triangle separating them from the roadway. Enemy bombers had struck Wyke Regis in the early hours of 28 June 1942, destroying a number of buildings in Shrubbery Lane, including the centuries-old Ship Inn where the landlord's wife was among five killed in the attack.

Almost fifty years on, this scene is difficult to pin-point today but the narrowness of the lane and the house on the left suggest that this must be Collins Lane off the High Street at Wyke Regis where modern properties stand today. Just beyond the trees in the background can be seen the Wyke House Hotel, this site also now redeveloped as Wooland Gardens.

It was not only on Commercial Road that vehicles and pedestrians could find themselves held up by trains, although on Abbotsbury Road at Westham there was a subway for those on foot and in a hurry. This was Littlefield level crossing on the Weymouth and Portland Railway, with the crossing keeper's cottage on the left. The train was a 'special' on the last run to Portland in March 1965 when the line officially closed.

A night-time scene which includes a view of the laundry which once stood in Abbotsbury Road (adjacent to the shops on the right). It opened as the Weymouth Sanitary Steam Laundry Co. in Victorian times, and its establishment in the newly developing suburb led to facetious suggestions that Westham would perhaps be better called 'Washington'. The laundry was demolished in the 1970s, initially to make way for a petrol station but the houses of Swallow Court have now been built on the site.

Difficult to see this view today as the hedge in the centre of the photograph is now some 3m (10ft) high. On the left is Chickerell Road as it approaches the traffic lights at Benville Road. The buildings are those of May Farm.

The first new post-war public house built in Weymouth opened on 15 December 1958, the Admiral Hardy at Westham Crossroads. Architects of the Purbeck-stone pub were Crickmay & Sons of Weymouth. The name commemorates Nelson's famous flag-captain and Admiral, Sir Thomas Masterman Hardy, who was born at Portesham, and was chosen from 1600 competition entries, two winners sharing first prize. The licence for the new Eldridge Pope hostelry was transferred from the brewery's closed Lamb and Flag pub in Lower Bond Street and 'mine host' was Joseph Meakin, former licensee of the Lamb and Flag.

Known as 'Fiveways', this junction on Chickerell Road is now traffic-light controlled. The garage in Benville Road has been extended by a modern structure and houses fill more of the background fields between Lanehouse and Wyke.

'Alf's' is still on the corner of Lynch Road and Chickerell Road but occupants of the other shops in this 1950s development have changed over the years. This area of the borough remained relatively rural until after the First World War, when the expansion of the town at Westham began to stretch out along the road to Chickerell. Previously farmland, this corner was known as 'Iron Box', the name apparently derived from the stone and galvanised iron milking shed which stood right on the corner shown. The building in the centre of the photograph is the old farmhouse. It became home to Mr Alfonso Forte (of the Forte hotel chain family and Forte's ice cream parlour formerly on the corner of Westham Road) who was, of course, the original 'Alf' of the fish and chip shop.

The establishment of the Lynch Lane Industrial Estate to the west of the town was part of a drive to attract light industry to Weymouth in the immediate post-war years. Bristol's Instrument Company moved into this new factory in December 1948, producing precision recording instruments. The firm's name was that of the company's American founder, a Professor Bristol; the firm moved to Weymouth from the London area. Another London company, Elliott Bros., took over from Bristol's but transferred its business to Kent in 1958. Telerection occupied the site for many years afterwards.

Bristol's Instruments staff 'At work(!)...'

...and 'At Play'. Carnival procession fun in 1953.

Lanehouse Rocks Road photographed on a bleak wintry day in January 1963. Today's garage, rebuilt, is on the same site. Beyond it are the 1950s houses of the Littlesea Estate. Later building developments took houses up the hill towards Wyke Regis and also filled the fenced area opposite the service station.

As the demand for new houses increased in the years following the end of the Second World War, the suburb of Lanehouse expanded rapidly. By 1948 work on building the council estates was well under way. In the late 1950s the Littlesea Estate Company began developing land on the opposite side of Lanehouse Rocks Road. This was no speculative venture. Houses were built to order only and to keep costs down these traditional-style homes were constructed to a standard pattern.

The concrete pillars and electrical gear of this small switching station stood behind the once extensive buildings of East Chickerell Court Farm. The 300-acre farm was beyond the Wessex Stadium, between Radipole and Chickerell. Its buildings were allowed to fall into disrepair in the mid-1960s when the Central Electricity Generating Board announced plans for the erection of a 50-acre sub-station site here. A public inquiry overruled objections to the plans and the farm disappeared to make way for the present transformer station.

The Universal Engineering Company acquired these workshops at Charlestown from Southern National in 1959. The bus company had used the building as a paint shop and store prior to the rebuilding of the Edward Street bus station in the early fifties, the original bus garage having been destroyed in a Second World War bombing raid. Universal Engineering was then opposite what is now Charlestown Motors (then Yarlands Service Station). The houses in the background still stand, but Universal Engineering has transferred to the Granby Industrial Estate and these premises on the Chickerell Road were demolished, making way for the houses of Lloyd Terrace.

Landlord Dan Crewe is seen surrounded by the vast collection of militaria which once decorated the public bar of the Alexandra Inn at Charlestown. On show were more than 400 badges, shoulder flashes, swords, bayonets, knives and daggers. The Alexandra was also known for the murals of Dorset scenes on the walls of its public and lounge bars, painted by Mr Crewe. He and his wife Nan retired from the licensed trade in 1966.

Portland Beach Road as it enters the island, viewed from the shingle of Chesil Beach in 1956. A busy railway scene with numerous wagons in the sidings. The Weymouth and Portland Railway had carried its last regular passengers in 1952 and would be goods-only until its closure in 1965. Beyond the Mere some of the Navy's extensive playing fields would be tarmaced over in the late 1950s when the Naval Heliport was built. In the background (far right) much of the former RN Hospital has now been demolished.

The layout and seating arrangements clearly show that this was once a cinema, converted to bingo as film-going audiences declined. Formerly the Regal cinema at Fortuneswell, Portland, it was the last of the island's three cinemas to close. The photograph was taken in the early 1980s. The building burned down in the 1990s.

A touch of the high life for Weymouth arrived in the late 1960s with the opening of the Lodmoor House Gaming Casino. It was a substantial change of use for the building which in Victorian times had been a school for young gentlewomen! Lodmoor House, as Lodmoor High School, flourished until the 1930s, becoming the Lodmoor House Hotel then holiday flatlets in post-war years. Currently the mid-nineteenth century house is Avon-Lea, a residential and nursing home.

Knight & Daughter's Australian Food Fortnight got off to a good start in July 1961 with a visit from a bush ranger and a kangaroo! On the corner of Alexandra Road and Dorchester Road at Lodmoor Hill, this is now a charity shop.

More than thirty years ago this sylvan scene could be found quite close to town, on the Dorchester Road at its junction with Waverley Road. The then-unmade road led to a small industrial development which still exists today. These wooded grounds surrounded Nos 211 and 213 Dorchester Road, demolished in the late 1960s. The apartments of Holly Court now fill the site.

At its far end Waverley Road (fortunately now tarmaced) overlooks the railway. The Patrick Engineering Co. Ltd. (facing, centre) still occupies the same site today.

In 1955 Weymouth's new police station replaced cramped and unsuitable accommodation in the town centre's Guildhall. Now this Dorchester Road building is also redundant. In 2001 the divisional police headquarters relocated to new offices at Southill. A smaller building on the Dorchester Road site serves this area of Weymouth and the site pictured here will be redeveloped as housing.

Nothing is recognisable today in this 1955 Dorchester Road scene. No. 148 (right) was then the Weymouth depot of motor coach proprietors Bere Regis & District Motor Services, their vehicles in livery of two shades of brown being a familiar sight all over Dorset. Next came Hayward's Yard where local dyers and dry cleaning firm A.E. Sams Ltd had its factory. On the far left can be seen a little relic of the old toll road days, the Radipole tollhouse, demolished in 1976. In later years various car dealerships occupied the area shown here before it was redeveloped by the Lidl supermarket chain.

Bere Regis Garage, Dorchester Road in 1955, with a typical stone 'garage-style' façade. Day-trips by coach were on offer to places as far afield as Looe and Polperro (8am–10 pm) for 19s.6d, or Portsmouth and Southsea (9am–10pm) for 14s.6d.

The scene in 1957 at Skew Bridge, which takes Dorchester Road over the railway at Radipole, is a little less rural today. Many of the trees have gone and a steel footbridge added to the right-hand side offers protection to pedestrians on this busy main road.

Almost forty years have passed since these photographs were taken at Radipole Spa. Bignell's is now converted to residential use and the Summit Stores is an Indian takeaway.

A development at the top end of Radipole Lake in 1957; these houses are being built in Grasmere Road. The choice of street names on a Lake District theme continues the tradition of the earlier developments here, the names of famous lakes presumably being thought fitting for the local lakeside homes.

One of those attractive, unchanging scenes. St Ann's Church and the Old Manor, Radipole in 1958.

Traditional offerings and decorations for harvest festival at St Ann's Church, Radipole, in 1954.

The late-sixteenth century Old Manor, Radipole. The house, some parts of which are of even earlier date, stands beside the churchyard of St Ann's.

St Aldhelm's Church in Spa Road today looks very different from this photograph of 1954. A large extension now runs along the front of the building, with a decorated fascia above. Opened in 1940, St Aldhelm's is a sister church to Radipole's St Ann's, the tiny Parish Church proving too small to accommodate the growing community.

A new primary school opened in Radipole in 1965 to replace the little village school opposite St Ann's Church in Radipole Lane.

One of the new school's class-rooms in December 1966.

North Mill, Mill Street, Broadwey in its productive days. The mill was converted to residential use in the late 1960s. First registered in January 1944, the Austin K2 type lorry was new to Wright's, the owners of the mill. By the time this photograph was taken in 1954 the lorry had lost its wartime headlight masks and had been repainted in the Meech livery, new owners of Broadwey Mill.

Very little to recognise in this Broadwey scene today. The garage opposite the end of Old Station Road has been completely rebuilt and the attractive art-deco style dwelling which stood on the site in 1958 has since been demolished.

Dorchester Road at Broadwey in 1966. Lockwood the butcher's shop has been converted to a house, as has the Railway Station Hotel.

Almost forty years ago and the Dorchester Road at Upwey appears rural and almost traffic free. Devenish's Railway Station Hotel was still in business (since converted to housing) and Grays actually ran the shop at Grays Corner on the Old Station Road/Dorchester Road junction (today a veterinary practice). The flats of Cassea Court now occupy the tree-filled foreground site on the left.

A change of scene at Upwey. Shepstone's Garage on the Dorchester Road has been completely rebuilt and is now Wey Valley Motors. In the background is the Congregational church, now closed. The photograph was taken in 1966.

Watery Lane, Upwey living up to its name in the floods of July 1955.

The Royal Oak was the last building on the south side of the Dorchester Road at Upwey, before the long climb up Ridgeway. Two years after this photograph was taken, during the snow and ice of the 1962/63 winter, the pub was demolished and road visibility improved at this spot.

Three early sunseekers (this was May 1966) relax on Preston Beach amid the untidy jumble of piles which were one of many unsuccessful attempts to keep the sea at bay here. Frequent flooding on Preston Beach Road and consequent traffic disruption led to the construction of the present sea defence wall in the 1990s. The erosion of Furzy Cliffs in the background had also long been a problem. The end house of the row of coastguard cottages shown here slid into the sea in 1970. Extensive work to combat these slippages was carried out in the early 1980s.

This garage site at Overcombe Corner has been redeveloped as housing, as has the area to the right where cars are parked. This scene, taken in July 1967, is still overlooked by the 'Embassy Hotel' (now the Spyglass Inn) and the coastguard cottages, although land slippage took the end of this block down the cliff.

For many years the Spyglass Inn at Overcombe was the 'Embassy Hotel', as in this photograph from the early 1950s. The area below the old coastguard cottages has been substantially redeveloped and since the mid-1990s the new sea wall has provided an attractive walk from this corner to the Esplanade, harbourside and pier.

It was quite an event when Mayor Edgar Wallis opened the Solid Fuel Show House on the Weymouth Bay Estate at Preston in May 1961. This was a National Coal Board central-heating promotion. The Show House (actually a bungalow) is in Oakbury Drive where, in 1961, prices for one of the homes on the new estate started at £3225.

In the early 1960s Chappell's Garage stood at the junction of Preston Road and Seven Acres Road at Preston. Later taken over by other garage proprietors, the building was finally removed and the apartments of Whitelee Court were built here in the late 1980s.

In the fifty years since this photograph was taken, the Bridge Inn at Preston has been considerably enlarged. There is now an extension to the front of the building, which is no longer thatched.

It is hard to believe that these attractive cottages beside an idyllic village pond at Sutton Poyntz in the 1960s were tumbledown ruins overlooking a weed-choked stretch of water a decade earlier.

The Sutton Poyntz cottages and overgrown pond before restoration work began.

More winter problems! Snow on the Littlemoor Road on 3 January 1963.

The South Dorset Hunt at Osmington Mills in 1957 when today's Smuggler's Inn was the Picnic Inn.

Warmwell Crossroads was a notorious accident blackspot in the 1950s, despite the removal of hedges and trees to improve visibility. This view, taken in 1955, looks towards Weymouth. The eventual solution was the construction of the roundabout here in 1959.

Despite protestations in the late 1950s from Ringstead residents that proposed 120ft high USAF radio antennae would be a blot on the landscape, the Air Ministry was permitted to acquire the land required for them by compulsory purchase and construction began. The two dish-shaped reflective antennae stood here until 1975, and can be seen in the background of this coastal scene. Part of a worldwide communications network, the dishes became redundant as satellite technology took over and the USAF base, which controlled them, moved out in 1973. The dishes can be seen in close up in *Weymouth: The Golden Years*, page 160.

At the entrance to Chaldon Herring is the village pub, The Sailor's Return, which provided the title for author David Garnett's avant-garde novel of 1928. Garnett's body was brought back from France on his death in 1981 for burial in the churchyard at Chaldon Herring. The pub has been considerably extended since this photograph of 1961 but retains much of its early-nineteenth-century character.

Chaldon Herring, also known as East Chaldon, is a remote and unspoiled village which lies between Winfrith and the coast, a tiny place but with a wealth of literary and artistic associations. The Powys brothers lived and wrote here, and Theodore Powys' classic novel *Mr Weston's Good Wine* is set in the village, renamed Folly Down in the story. Llewelyn Powys and his writer wife Alyse Gregory were here in the 1920s and 30s. His ashes are buried on the clifftop nearby, the spot marked by an inscribed block of Portland stone. Hope Muntz wrote her best-known novel *The Golden Warrior* at Chaldon Herring where her sister, sculptor Elizabeth Muntz, had her studio. Writers Sylvia Townsend Warner and Valentine Ackland are buried in the churchyard. Today the red telephone box and rustic pillarbox still stand outside this row of thatched cottages.

This is Canadian-born sculptor Elizabeth Muntz outside the row of cottages where she lived and worked from 1938 until her death in 1977. On the cliffs at White Nothe she set a block of inscribed Portland stone in memory of another famous Chaldon Herring resident:
Llewelyn Powys
13th Aug 1884
2nd Dec 1939
The living. The living.
He shall praise Thee.

At the far end of the village the church of St Nicholas is of Norman origin, rebuilt in the medieval period and altered in the nineteenth century. From this high point can be seen the ridge of ancient burial barrows known as the 'Five Marys'.

For a number of years Elizabeth Muntz ran a summer school of sculpture, painting and pottery at Chaldon Herring. Here her students find inspiration on the cliffs above Bat's Head in 1955.

Elizabeth Muntz at work in Chaldon Herring. There are a number of examples of her work in Dorset. These include a series of beautiful carved stone mural panels designed for Weymouth's first new post-war school, Broadwey Modern School, opened in 1948 (now Wey Valley School).

It is difficult to appreciate the beauty and size of this magnificent sculpture on its site 15m (50ft) above the ground. 'Erst' weighs 3½ tons and is one of two figures designed for Winfrith Atomic Energy Research Establishment by Eric Morris. The figure (its name is Anglo-Saxon for 'first') shows a Herculean man breaking shackles, symbolising the forcing asunder of the nucleus of the atom. A second figure, 'Forthward' symbolised progress in scientific research. Both were the work of the Sutton Poyntz sculptor whose work can be seen in several Dorset schools and churches (including a sculpture in the grounds of Wyke Regis Infants' School). Eric Morris died in 1960.

This Portesham, scene has changed little since 1957, apart from the change of use of the Half Moon Inn building; the pub, now closed, has been converted to a private house.

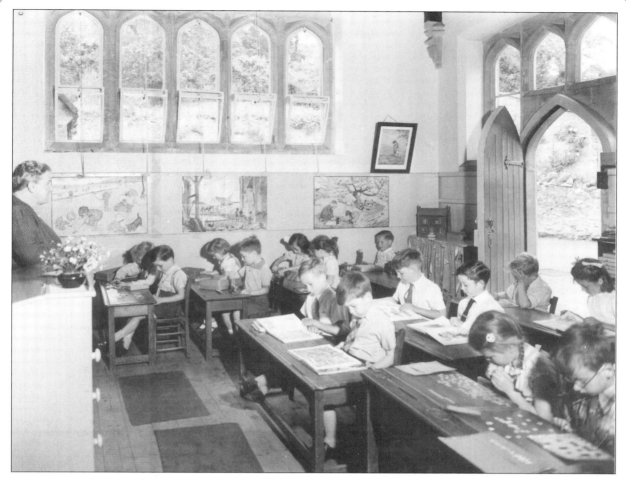

A picture celebrating the centenary of the village school at Abbotsbury in 1958. Sadly, the latter years of the twentieth century saw the closure of a number of these small rural schools and this one taught its last pupil in the early 1980s. Its building, though, is still well used as a community centre, the Strangways Hall, in the middle of the village.

Standing 9m (30ft) above the water, this oil rig appeared some two-and-a-half miles out from Lulworth in September 1963 as the British Petroleum Exploration Company sought to find a site as productive as that at Kimmeridge. It was not to be. The 750m (2500ft) borehole produced only a small non-marketable oil supply and a negligible amount of gas. Six weeks later the rig was removed.

That icy winter of 1962/63, the 'big freeze', brought Siberian conditions to much of Dorset. Here, attempts are being made to clear the Old Sherborne Road after fresh snowfalls in February 1963.

This superb stone carving of the Dorset coat-of-arms was produced by Adams & Mitchell, monumental masons of Portland. The grant of arms to Dorset County Council was made on 21 February 1950. Why 'Who's Afear'd'? The motto originated in Dorset, being that of the Society of Dorset Men. In the early 1900s when the Society was founded with a modest membership, Thomas Hardy suggested 'Who's afraid' or 'Who's afear'd' to prove that Dorset would not be overshadowed by similar societies in larger counties.